BULLIED: HOW I GOT BY...

Short stories by people who have
lived to tell about it, literally

Lonnee Rey & Friends

Lonnee Rey

To all the isolated demoralized people out there - this book will give you hope, healing and probably a few laughs.

This is how we hope to change the world for all of us, but especially you...come on back out and join us in the movement to end bullying, once and FOR ALL.

CONTENTS

FOREWORD BY DR. MARCIA THOMAS… FROM DIAPER TO DYSFUNCTION

As parents, our greatest desire is to raise children who are loving, compassionate, kind, considerate and emphatic. Yet despite our best efforts and intentions, we may unwittingly nurture bullies in our own homes. The subtle ways we do this can be astonishing. It's time to shed light on these hidden patterns, habits and routines.

In our desire to fulfill our divine calling as parents to protect and empower our children we often succumb to their every need- thus inadvertently programming them from birth to adulthood to prioritize their own needs above others. We often dismiss and downplay their hurtful, disrespectful and aggressive behaviors. The undeniable fact is that our parenting styles can either nurture empathy and inclusion or promote an unbalanced self-love or survival mode that manifests itself as uncontrolled aggression.

When you consistently downplay or ignore your child's mean behavior towards a sibling and ignore the unkind jokes, teasing and taunts with the excuse that they are 'just having fun or joking,' the child learns that hurtful behavior is acceptable and persons who take offense are overly sensitive or unreasonable. Even worse, is the instances where we become overly protective of our child's feelings by refusing to allow our child to apologize or make amends when they hurt someone or consistently intervening and shielding your child from consequences or challenges and always steps in to resolve conflicts for your child.

When you constantly compare your child to others or their siblings labeling them as smart or gifted, your child develops a competitive mindset, feeling the need to always be better than or ahead of others, potentially resulting in bullying behavior. Using our power and control to manipulate or exploit our children to get what we want, yelling, or using physical force to get others and our child to comply with our wishes encourages our children to mirror that behavior and see bullying as an effective way to get people to do what we want and achieve their goals.

These patterns often unintentionally back your child against the lack of empathy wall and makes your child struggle to understand, respect and accept others perspectives. Additionally, the child develops a sense of entitlement and is unable to cope with failure or adversity, leading to increased aggression and entitlement.

"Children who are allowed to have their own way, and are indulged in their desires, will soon become discordant notes in the family, and will be a source of trouble and annoyance to all around them." – Ellen G. White

T his book will challenge you to examine your practices and discover the subtle ways you may be nurturing bullies. It will encourage you to reflect on your own experiences and explore the hidden dynamics of bullying, the bully, the victim and the bystander. You will gain a deeper understanding of the devastating impact on individuals, in institutions, families and the broader society. We will learn how together we can break the cycle of bullying and raise a generation who will create a more inclusive, supporting and loving space on this earth. The journey begins.

Meet Dr. Marcia Thomas, an accomplished published author, certified Christian professional leadership consultant, trainer and Christian strategic Life Coach is an anti-bullying advocate who has spearheaded a parenting program aimed at helping parents to understand how unintentional parenting choices can contribute to the development of bullying behaviors.

With over two decades of experience as a Christian instructional leader and administrator across varying levels within the education sector, community and church settings, she has amassed profound insights on how to navigate the complexities inherent in leadership roles. Driven by a passion to empower others, she established MTS Consulting and Coaching, a center committed to supporting faith based introverted female leaders and professionals in their quest for personal development and advancement.

As an adept introverted female leader, Dr. Thomas possesses a nuanced understanding of the distinct challenges and strengths inherent of introverted personalities particularly within the realms of life and professional ministry. Drawing from her extensive background, she offers tailored support to individuals seeking to navigate life challenges and leadership and thrive both personally and professionally.

In addition to her coaching and consultancy work, Dr. Thomas has five publications to her credit. Her latest book 'A Leader Like You' is a testament to her expertise and is available for purchase on Amazon, https://a.co/d/0o49gWN, offering invaluable insights and practical guidance for Christian and secular leaders.

INTRODUCTION

We know bullying events can trigger a person. Our intention is to make this book valuable to everyone, whether or not the actual stories are read right away. This book is not a dumpster full of trauma you need to sift through to find the nuggets of wisdom.

In fact, we believe you can read this book in about 15 mins., and not get triggered by difficult stories.

Here is how:

At the top of each story is:
"Hey, Allison, what I really want you to know is ___."
It will give you the gist of the story.

"Allison" is a fictious person we addressed in the beginning of each chapter. She is reminiscent of Alice in Wonderland who dealt with The Queen of Hearts, a bully if there ever was one.

At the bottom of each story you will find *******
This is the wrap-up, the lessons, advice and insights each writer wanted you to know as to how they "got by."

Skim the chapters to get the message and the insights.

The only exception is "Bullies took our babies," by Trine and Vidar, who wrote letters to their missing children.

We have shared the many faces of bullying, separated into categories, so you can use the book like a reference tool. If ever the day comes that you feel alone, or wonder how the heck you can heal from a bullying experience, the short stories here will keep you company...show that you are not the only one...no, you are not to blame...nor are you losing your mind.

We have all been 'through it' with bullies, as you will soon see. This is how we got over it.

Never has there been a more dedicated and passionate assembly of writers who want to end bullying once and FOR ALL, literally.

Reach out to them. Please. They are here to help you. If you found their story moving, tell them.

We hope you will breeze through our book, at first, and recommend it to others, next. In this way, we are ships rising together in the tides of positive change.

The views expressed here are solely those of each author and not representative of the group as a whole. However, every one of us stands behind one message: "Stop Bullying" only means something if we do something.

We want you to feel empowered to take back authority over your life, and summons the courage to be the change you seek in your lifetime. You deserve it, and our world needs you to stand tall, in your power, and actualize the mighty spirit within you because you were born to do great things.

May you be blessed with such passionate supporters as
the writers you are about to read!

We look forward to knowing you, too, dear one.

Lonnee Rey
Editor

A PRIMER ON BULLYING

Bullying is a complex issue. However, there are some common traits and characteristics of bullying that can be seen in all types. What follows is a depiction of the commonalities inherent in bullying. All of the stories told in the pages of this book have at least one, if not multiple, common characteristics of bullying woven throughout their story.

Here is a bully primer/overview of things you need to know to help you get by more effectively.

These stories are raw and honest. Read on, though difficult. You will feel supported and not alone. The effects of bullying stay with you for a lifetime. Some current experiences and memories will trigger you and take you on that emotional roller coaster that only those who have been bullied can understand.

These stories aim to change a culture where bullying is so common that it's viewed as almost 'normal,' but it should never be.' – Choi Si-won.

Memories or experiences that remind us of a time we were victimized and bullied do not mean we have not healed. That's a bunch of b*******! Healing is not synonymous with never being reminded or affected by an experience that runs so deep it changes your "DNA."

There is much more you need to understand about

being a victim of bullying. People tend to say trite comments including: ignore them; don't react; don't respond because that is what the bullies want. Don't give them what they want. Get over it. Why do you care what they think or say? You are making them important, and you need to stop. Bullies bully because they don't feel good about themselves, so they bully others to make themselves feel better.

Oh, really? Somehow, people think that is supposed to make you feel honored to be the recipient of bullying. *You hate yourself, so you torture me,* said no one ever.

Your experience being bullied is 100% real and true. Just because others try to minimize it doesn't mean it can or should be minimized. Being bullied changed you at your core. The scars left by bullying take years to overcome and may not be wholly or entirely gone, ever.

Few people know how much bullying leads people to become people-pleasers and introverts who try to avoid confrontation. Bullying makes you feel worthless, like the world would be better off without you; lonely, sad, and isolated. Being bullied causes many to retreat and give in to what others want, losing self-worth, -confidence, -respect, sanity, family, friends, and dignity. Bullies want you to feel all of these things and will do all they can to keep you isolated from friends and family. They want you to feel small, invalidated, and even silly for feeling hurt by them. Over time, your diminished self-worth compounds so badly that isolation is your best move.

You don't have to stay silent when bullying happens. You can and should say something. Firstly, staying quiet doesn't stop bullying; it often intensifies it because the bullies continue to "up the ante" until they have gotten a response from the bullied. Secondly, when you say something, it's not about gaining the bully's understanding or compassion. It is about standing up for yourself and your self-worth and protecting your self-esteem and self-confidence.

"Brave" by Sara Bareilles

"You can be amazing
You can turn a phrase into a weapon or a drug.
You can be the outcast.
Or be the backlash of somebody's lack of love.
Or you can start speaking up.
Nothing's gonna hurt you the way that words do
When they settle 'neath your skin
Kept on the inside and no sunlight
Sometimes, a shadow wins.
But I wonder what would happen if you

Say what you wanna say
And let the words fall out.
Honestly, I wanna see you be brave"

Thirdly, when you are bullied, try to stay focused on goals and dreams that are important to you. Don't let the bully's behavior distract or deter you from reaching those goals/dreams.

Many profess that they want to end bullying, and yet it's still a conversation they are afraid to have for fear of retaliation. People would still prefer to join the bully rather than rally around the bullied person.

You are not the cause of the problem. Seeking help is not a sign of weakness but rather of strength. Don't let your only regret be not seeking professional help sooner to feel healthier.

If there is a next time: Don't try to be a people-pleaser, and don't be afraid of disagreement or confrontation to the point of not speaking up. By no longer being silenced, you will have a better chance at restoring, or retaining, your self-worth, -esteem, -confidence, -respect, sanity, family, friends, and dignity.

Let's call a spade a spade. Being a victim of bullying is not easy or pleasurable. It is downright hell. Everybody involved in this project hopes that this primer, along with all the stories told between the pages of this book, empowers victims of bullying and inspires those who align with the bullies to make a shift, stand tall, switch camps, and refuse to support any type of bullying behavior. We believe that then and only then will bullying be on the road to becoming extinct.

Some common signs of professional bullying include:

- Being constantly criticized or belittled

- Being excluded from meetings or decisions

- Being given unrealistic tasks or deadlines

- Being subjected to verbal abuse or intimidation

- Being humiliated or embarrassed in front of colleagues

- Being sabotaged or having their work undermined

Bullying in the workplace, bullying in care facilities, and in abusive relationships, typically has its origins in childhood aggression that was never properly addressed. While overt bullying tends to change as people get older (becoming more subtle and manipulative), it rarely ever goes away on its own…and the effects can be deadly.

After Daughter Takes Her Life, Dad Sends An Invitation To Her Bullies

Kate and Tick Everett founded Dolly's Dream in memory of Dolly, who took her own life after an extended period of bullying and cyberbullying. They're now focused on preventing other families from going through the same experience.

Dolly's father invited the bullies to his 14 year old daughter's funeral so they could see the results of their relentless bullying. This short video, highlighting a beautiful young girl's modeling career, exuberant attitude toward life, involvement in sports, and the aftermath of her suicide, might be used as a teaching tool. It is beyond-time for bullies to face consequences and be held accountable for their actions, don't you think?

Here is Dolly's drawing, taken from the short video, which you can watch here: *After Daughter Takes Her Life, Dad Sends An Invitation To Her Bullies*

https://youtu.be/pQ3U5usBpK0?si=9-87s5zYhebHR2JV

SPEAK EVEN IF YOUR VOICE SHAKES

After Daughter Takes Her Life, Dad Sends An Invitation To Her Bullies.
SPEAK EVEN IF YOUR
VOICE SHAKES

SCHOOL

SHARON BIRN…SCHOOL DAZE

Hey, Allison, what I really want you to know is people will try to minimize your feelings around your experience of being bullied when it comes to groups and cliques at school.

It began in middle school and continued throughout high school. It was relentless, every day, from the moment I entered the building until I arrived home. Thank goodness for me, technology and cyber-bullying had not entered society yet. I'm not sure I would have survived.

I was born with a disability, and have been confined to a wheelchair my entire life. Kids thought it was funny to empty their garbage into my school bag, destroying my books, homework, and personal belongings. If that weren't bad enough, they would write me "love notes" aimed at destroying my self-esteem, with mean spirited comments about my weight, my clothes, my wheelchair, etc. They would also steal my textbooks and notebooks, which meant that if they could not be found, I would have to buy new books and do all the work over for the marking period we were in, or (to quote my supportive teachers), "I would have no grade, as they would have nothing to grade me on."

I would be invited to parties only to sit by myself and have snack food to "keep me company" while kids were off in cliques talking about me. How did I know? They would sometimes look in my direction and laugh. They would jump on the back of my chair, forcing it to almost tip over, as they would jump down and watch and laugh while I got startled and screamed in fear.

I remember being so excited when, as a preteen girl, I finally got invited to a slumber party. As expected, with nightfall we all got in our pajamas. Some chose to sit on the couch, while others, like myself, lay on the floor in their sleeping bags. I already just wanted it to be over, having spent most of the night as I had at other parties: sitting in the corner with snack foods as company. I remember thinking it can't get much worse than this. Boy, was I wrong!

Although I felt tired, I could not get comfortable enough to fall asleep, so I just closed my eyes. I then heard one of the girls say "Is she sleeping?" I listened to another girl respond, "I think so, I'm pretty sure." The next thing I knew, I became that party's subject matter and the laughingstock. I became the topic of conversation from that moment throughout the rest of the night until morning. I heard the leader say "Sharon is so fat that all she ever does is eat. Can you believe how much candy she ate? For lunch every day, she brings a bagel with either tuna fish or egg salad..." Nothing was off-limits as more girls joined in, talking about my wheelchair, how I wore my hair, my clothes, and anything else they could think of about me that would keep them in good standing with the bully/leader. One girl stayed silent through most of the conversation and briefly came to my defense but quickly returned to silence when she became a 'shooting range' for the bully's target practice.

My social life throughout school taught me that it's easier for people to align with the bully to avoid retaliation or retribution, which is guaranteed to occur if they align with the bullied person.

****

How did I get by? I always had two primary goals for my future: to be a mom and to help others. To do both those things, I knew I would require a higher education. I want to support myself and my family and help people as I envisioned. The bullies had already taken everything else: my self-worth, self-confidence, self-esteem, and hardest of all, my dignity. I would not let them take my goals and future from me. By staying focused on my goals and getting excellent grades, I could get a degree that would allow me to help others and earn enough to support my future family.

There is one last thing that I want you to know or remind you of. One way that bullies keep their power is to keep their victims silent. If you are being bullied, I want to encourage you and inspire you to keep talking and speaking out against the bullying you are experiencing until you find someone who truly listens and will help.

For those of you who might be reading this who are accomplices to the bullying and want to protect yourself from being the bully's next victim, I encourage you and challenge you to take a much more courageous approach. Rather than aligning with the bully, align with the person being bullied. There is strength in numbers. Take the power away from the bully and give it back to everyone else!

Sharon Birn is a transformational life coach, multiple number-one best-selling co-author, and riveting public speaker who helps moms and their children beat burnout, enabling them to thrive. As a single mom to her son and a dog mom to Minnie, Sharon profoundly understands the challenges and joys of family life. Her speaking engagements are highly sought after, leaving participants feeling empowered and capable. Sharon's presentations cover crucial topics that impact today's families. Her work emphasizes giving mental health the same priority, attention, and respect as physical health. She helps her clients rise above their past circumstances to design abundant lives by focusing on their abilities, assets, talents, and gifts rather than the perceived faults and deficits others believe true. In her anthology contribution, Sharon shares her experiences of being bullied in all phases of life and provides readers with strategies on how she got by.

 https://www.linkedin.com/in/sharon-birn-9a4a5792/
http://www.possibilitiesrinfinite.com

TREVOR MARTIN…
LOCKED AND LOADED

Hey Allison what I want you to know is it gets better….

*Oh n fuck the critics, let 'em hate, just make
sure they spell your name right.*

Light shines on my face. It's coming through the three slits in the locker door. It's your typical 90's era, high school locker designed more for backpacks, folders, gym shoes, and books than my 125 lb freshman ass. I blink... trying to hold back tears. I hate these tears trying to make their way out onto my cheeks. They mean that I am about to cry, and that means I'm weak. I hate being weak. I squeeze my eyes shut so hard that my head starts to hurt. I just want to dig a hole, crawl into it and never come out. My feet are starting to cramp so I try to move around but that doesn't go well. It's slippery inside this locker. The bottom of it is wet. It's covered in piss...and it's not my piss. You see Kevin has had a bad day... and when Kevin has a bad day, I have a bad day.

It was quick. Not painless, but quick, nonetheless. Locker door was open, I was grabbing my books for the next class, and thinking about how I really didn't want to go home (ironic considering my current situation in this locker) after the final bell. I never heard Kevin coming. His forearm hit the back of my head and the left side of my face hit steel. I tried to blink the stars away as I felt his hand grab reach around and grab the front of my shirt. His breath smelled like chew...minty and sweet. The tobacco peeked out at me, as he started to grin. "Hey man...are those new shoes?" I turned my head as far as I could to follow his gaze into my open locker to the shoes in question.

Black Reeboks. Brand new. I was looking forward to wearing them during gym class. Kevin apparently had other plans. I gulped and tried to breathe as he held me against the lockers. "Hey, you little fucker did you not hear me?" I nodded that I heard him, but he didn't care. His mind was already made up. The plan had already been greenlit, and we were GO. He let go of me and pointed a tobacco smudged finger in my face. "Stay the fuck still, Slim or I'll cave your Adams apple in." I believed him. You see, I had witnessed Kevin beat the shit out of another "slim" before. He wasn't kidding. He had the ability to make any of us "slims" piss our pants just by shouting "Hey you!! Yeah you, you little fucker!" So yeah, I believed him.

I stood frozen as he reached inside my locker. His smile grew even bigger as his hands closed around the Reeboks. "Oh…yeah these are nice. I know what I am going to do with these "slim". I knew it was a bad idea to remind him that they were my shoes, and I had plans for them, but against my better judgment I opened my mouth. "Hey man, uhhh yeah listen, I just got those, and I really like them…and well ummm I want to wear them for gym." Kevin stopped smiling. "What the fuck did you just say slim?" he said as he spit inside my locker. "Listen you little fucker, I knnnowww you didn't just open your stupid-ass mouth and say something to me." I looked at the floor. FUCK!! What had I done! I just poked the Kevin the "bear", that's what the fuck I had done. I thought, maybe if I avoid eye contact, he would forgive me for overstepping…turns out…. I was wrong.

Hands clasped around my throat so tight, my breath was gone in an instant. His angry eyes were right in front of mine. "Don't you ever fucking think that you can talk to me…EVER," he whispered. "You are pathetic, I mean just look at you. Slim ain't nobody gonna help you so shut the fuck up and get in the locker." I blinked and started to stutter... "Listen Kevin, just take the shoes, ok. I'll just wear the ones I have on." Kevin's snarl got bigger as he stepped towards me "Slim...get...in...the...fucking...locker...before I put you there." I could feel my throat tighten as the saliva in my mouth dried up. I looked at the locker. It was so small. I knew I wasn't a big kid, but still 5' 10" 125 lbs was gonna be a hard sell. Placing one foot in, I maneuvered my head around the coat and backpack hook, before smashing the shit out of my American History book as I placed my other foot inside.

BANG...BANG... the sound of Kevin trying to slam my locker door shut rang down the high school hallways. My hand was in the way. Kevin didn't care. He cussed as the door dug into my skin. "Slim move your god damn hand or I'll break it off." I finally got my hand inside, and the door latched with one final BANG.

"Hey slim...these are really nice shoes. You care if I keep em." Kevin whispered through the slits at the top of the locker door. I rested my head against the inside of the door. "Fuck this guy." I thought, but when you're 125lbs soaking wet, thinking "Fuck this guy" only gets you put inside of a locker. I could hear Kevin moving outside of the locker and I was sure that he was trying on MY new shoes. That's when I heard what sounded like water running, but that didn't make sense, because there wasn't a water fountain by my locker and Kevin didn't have a drink in his hands when he hit me.

I tried to push against the locker, but Kevin had it held tight and it wouldn't budge. "Slim stay the fuck still, I'm working on something," Kevin mutters. The sound of liquid starts...stops...trickles...then stops completely.

It dawns on me... but it's already too late. Kevin laughs as he takes one of my Reeboks full of his own piss and sloshes it against the top slits in the locker door.

My eyes burn, I taste salt as Kevin's hot urine runs down my face and neck soaking into my clothes. His laughter rings in my ears as he slams his fist against the door. "Hey slim, how's my piss taste you little bi..." ...the bell signifying class is over drowns out his voice as the hallways fill with kids heading to their lockers preparing for the next class.

Blinking rapidly, I try to wipe away the piss that is covering my face. It smells and is making it hard to get traction to stay still. If I am still enough maybe the kids with lockers on either side of me won't notice that I am in here and all will be quiet again. I close my eyes and try to plug my ears, hoping that if I can't see or hear them then they won't be there. Sound starts to fade away as my hands cover my ears. Spawn, my favorite comic book character, pops into my imagination, (damn near perfect timing I'd say.) You see, Spawn wasn't a bitch. Spawn wasn't a "slim." Spawn would have taken his chains and wrapped Kevin so tight that his body would have splattered all over the high school's walls.

The tears start to flow, and I start to hope that Kevin will come back and just finish the job. Thinking to myself definitely doesn't help... but fuck...should have seen this coming plain and simple... there is nothing about me that is relatable to these kids... different clothing, the stuttering....just different, and different gets bullied.

What was it that the bus driver said on my first day of high school when I stepped onto the bus? My mind drifts back....

It was Monday…not that that matters but I am pretty sure it was a Monday. Gotta be a Monday right, 'cuz let's be real, Monday's fucking suck. Anyways, on this specific day I was standing at the end of my driveway. Our house was on a gravel road so after this particular day, the lesson learned was that it is best to stand by the front of the house to avoid getting "dusted." Well, here I stand ready for the first day of high school. Clothes (white button up shirt and black slacks) are freshly pressed, my "man bag" (stitched in leather, cross included) is loaded to the gills with the usual school necessities, strap slung across my chest, satchel at my side and here we go!

The bus is about a quarter mile to the east. Palms start to get a bit sweaty as the nerves set in. Dad and Mom told me that this might happen and that God was on my side and would protect me in times of doubt. They said that I was protected by the full armor of God and could stand against the worldly armies of Satan. Somehow, I find confidence in this thought as the bus comes to a dusty halt in front of my house. The bus door swings open, and I take three steps up, putting me by the bus driver. As her hand reaches for the handle to close the door, the bus driver looks at me and stops mid motion. She shakes her head, sighs, and softly says, "Oh, you poor thing."

Back inside the high school locker my eyes snap open. THAT WAS IT!! That was what I was trying to remember, "Oh, you poor thing." The bus driver called it! She knew I was in for it… but how exactly? Was it the way I was dressed, was it my cross-stamped satchel? I shifted my weight inside the locker as the tears started again. Why did Kevin hate me so much? What had I done? What made him want to come after me?

The noise coming through the locker vents was the shuffle and chatter of students as they headed towards their lockers preparing for the next class. I held my breath praying that no one would notice the piss running out the bottom of mine. The rattle of my locker door caused me to jerk back as the door swung open, my head hitting the hook inside. "Fuck me" I muttered peering out into the hallway. Standing in front of me was another freshman... a girl, and she looked sad.

I looked at the floor. Eye contact was NOT happening. First it was a girl, second, I was covered in piss. "Hey, ummm hey are you ok" she asks. I don't reply. Maybe if I am quiet, she will just shut the door and leave me in here. Nope, no such luck. The girl squats down and whispers, "I'm not going to go get a teacher, but you really should get out of there. Let me help you," she says as she hands me a sweatshirt. "Take this...for your face" she says. Slipping out of the locker I grab the sweatshirt and start to dry off.

A numbness deep inside me has set in. The girl says, "Hey, you ok?" I look over, "Uh yeah I'll be ok, I just need to go to the bathroom," is my quiet response. As I start to walk down the hall, she comes up beside me and says, "Why don't I go to the lost and found and try and find you a different shirt? Maybe see if they have some sweatpants also?" I stop and turn to her, "Why are you doing this? Like, what do you want?" She doesn't balk. "I'm helping because no one deserves to be treated like this."

Nope, don't trust her. She's pretty and hangs out with some of the more popular kids. Silence is the best answer here, I think to myself heading into the boy's bathroom.

The mirror on the wall....fuck that mirror. My reflection

taunts me as paper towels full of Kevin's piss fall to the floor. God, I fucking hate Kevin. More than that, I hate me. I hate me for not standing up. I hate me because now a cute, no not cute, a HOT girl just saw me completely covered in someone else's piss. There is NO coming back from that. My hands grip the side of the sink as I try and rip it off the wall….but that's not possible… why…? Because I am a "slim" and let's be real…'weak, little slims' don't "rip" anything…ever.

"Hey, are you still in there?" calls out my would-be rescuer from the hallway. Shocked that she actually came back… my reply is a bit startled, "Umm yeah I am in here, uh, just cleaning up a bit, thanks." Silence hangs in the air as the internal struggle begins. I want those clothes, yet don't reeeaallly want to see her again. Hell, on that note, don't really care if I see anyone again….fucking ever. Somehow courage is mustered as this "slim" heads for the door. Turns out, clean clothes motivate me more than piss stains…who knew.

The girl is leaning against the wall opposite the boy's bathroom. She has one foot propped up against the locker's, an open book in one hand and clean clothes in the other. Noticing me, she slowly smiles as she hands me the clothes. "Hey, try these on, they should do the trick," she says as she crosses the hall. Taking the clothes I quickly head back into the bathroom. "I'll be right out here," she comments. "You don't have to, uh, I will be fine," is my short reply as I think, *Annndddd of course, I'm lying, there is no way in hell I will ever be "ok."*

The clothes fit…relieved, I shove the piss-stained clothes in the trash. There is a damn good chance when I get home, that I will get asked where they are, and why I am out of my usual apparel, but right now I give zero fucks about all that. The girl is waiting for me as I come out of the bathroom. "So, do you want to go to the office or tell anyone about this?" she asks. I shake my head "No" and head towards my locker. I have already missed 2 classes, and no one has come looking for me. It is clear that this institution also give zero fucks….about me.

The above narrative happened to me during my high-school years, and yeah it sucked… a lot. What did I learn from it? That bullies smell fear. They feed off of that shit. You show any sign of weakness, and they will latch on to it like a fucking parasite. Now, no one likes it when they are told they exude weakness. For instance, my father, who pulled no punches when I told him what happened to me. His direct response sent a crystal-clear message: you are picked on because you are weak. The bullying is actually your fault, because you refuse to stand up for yourself.

To be fair, he wasn't completely off the mark here. When asked if there was one thing that I could change about the story above what would it be, my response is always the same: stand my ground. Stand up for myself. Look those fuckers dead in the eye. No need to throw punches, but you can bet your ass I would not give one inch, NO not *one,* to the bully. That was the change needed.

Unfortunately for me, the choice to stand my ground was never made. Instead, comfort was found in my love for superheroes/heroines in the comics I would collect. Further conversation with my Dad was a moot point as he had stated his opinion and that was simply that. No need for further discussion. Mom followed Dad's lead and remained silent on the issue which then created a communicational rift. So, I went to where I felt safe and heard: my comics.

The masks those heroes/heroines could hide behind, their true identity disguised, like, how cool would that be?! The capes, body armor, savage face paint and BADASS vehicles... who wouldn't want to be one... or maybe have one, ya know ....as a friend...or even a best friend. Comic books could be found neatly stacked against the wall of my room, on my desk or even hidden in my school bag. (Remember, I didn't have a backpack) Ohhh, the adventures that happened right there in my room. Galaxies, multi-verses, and realm travel were all a possibility on any given afternoon...especially after school.

During school, well that was a totally different kind of shit show. The experience shared above was one of the many times that this ol' boy fell "victim" to the ever aggressive, ugly ass high school bully. Since it was clear that I was not going to be standing up for myself, protection would need to be found elsewhere. Once again, enter comics stage right. The pencil or pen became my "sword." Superheroes/heroines would come to life in the margins of notebooks as I would sketch them out creating stories of BADASS FIGHTS and BULLY BEAT DOWNS in my head (especially during Geography). This became the norm clear through my senior year. Heroes or Anti-heroes like Spawn, The Hulk, Deadpool, Wolverine and Ghost Rider would wage war on my behalf as I quickly skirted from classroom to locker, then back to classroom imagining that their sole mission was my survival.

I am 44 years old now and to this very day, those heroes and heroines can still be found in the pages of my notebooks at work, and on my drawing tablet at home. On my desk at my 9-5 sits a coffee mug, a special gift from my loving family of badass warriors. The front of the cup portrays Batman's grim crime fighting face staring back, reminding me that I am a force to be reckoned with and that I will give no quarter to any kind of bully. Now, you would think that this mug is used for an occasional cup o'joe. Well, you'd be wrong. For in this mug is housed a series of superhero Funko Pop Pens (Google it, they are legit) many of which were named above that still to this day are some of my closest friends...

.... Friends... that word has never been a big part of my life actually. I've never really had a lot of friends and to be honest with you, that is 100% my fault. You see, what you don't know but now will is that I became the very thing that I despised. A bully. As the years went on, my metabolism slowed and I learned that I could pack on muscle to the current 6 ' frame.

I can remember the feel of the cold bench press bar the first time it ever came off the rack. That fucker was heeeavvvyyy, but it felt good. Damn good. So good in fact, that over the next few years you could find me in the gym building myself up. Up to what you ask? A figure that no one, and I mean this, no one would dare bully again. The process had started and there was no turning back. What once was bullied would soon become the bully. Muscle and later on in life ink, would create a tapestry of narcissism the world did NOT need. A god like complex in formation that thrived on the fact that those that once shoulder checked me I the halls, now moved very quickly out of my fucking way. It was a sociopathic nightmare waiting to be unleashed... but that's another story for another time. (Foreshadowing here maybe- ahem... wink, wink.)

****

Now let's get back to the question at hand... the title of the book, how I got by....you ask me how I overcame the bullying back then? Two very important things - my mind and the POWERFUL act of love.

For those of you reading this that are experiencing bullying or have family members that are falling victim to it, know this: the mind is the most powerful thing in existence. Combine that with a splash of love, and you have yourself the recipe to overcome bullying and get through the darkest of days. As I close out this chapter, my challenge to you is this: Be the girl in my story. The one who opens the locker door. She was and is still a hero to me. Her name was Michelle and, in her memory, I want to leave you with this call to action...

The world is full of "Kevins." Don't be a Kevin, instead, strive every day to be a "Michelle" and pull people out of those lockers.

Meet Trevor Martin

An established and client-focused leadership coach, Trevor has 15 years of experience leading and coaching others. His passion for people and coaching is the driving force behind his success. He primarily works with entrepreneurs as they set and pursue goals, both in their personal and professional lives. Trevor's fierce passion and "Warrior Within" mindset, are the catalyst behind constant motivation, making him invaluable in his niche.

Trevor's interest in servant leadership began many years ago and motivated him to earn a degree in Criminal Justice. While his career led him to areas other than the Criminal Justice field, aspects of the curriculum served as a solid foundation to understanding people as he began working with leaders. In 2018, Trevor was introduced to the Values Based Leadership Program, and completed his Insights Discovery Profile thereafter. Trevor is active in his coaching practice, writing, public speaking on anti-bullying and promoting mental health.

https://www.linkedin.com/in/trevormartin-rmf/

https://www.youtube.com/@trevormartin_rmf23

SOCIAL SERVICES

HAAKON RIAN MANCIENT UELAND…SYSTEMIC BULLYING IN CHILD PROTECTIVE SERVICES: A CRITICAL EXAMINATION

Hey, Allison, you are not alone. There are legions of people who have lost custody to CPS under false pretenses. But the tides are changing.

I am Haakon Rian Mancient Ueland, Child Welfare Worker. In my chapter, I will share professional secrets for disarming bullies that you meet in social services, child welfare services and health care.

As a social worker with over two decades of experience, I have witnessed various forms of bullying, but none as egregious as the systemic bullying perpetrated by Child Protective Services (CPS) against vulnerable families. This chapter will delve into the case of Trine and Vidar, a Norwegian couple living in Sweden, who had their children taken away by CPS under false pretenses. I will share my professional insights and expertise to shed light on the unethical practices employed by CPS and the devastating consequences for families. And make suggestions on how you can improve your chances of a good solution, if you are in such a situation yourself.

Trine and Vidar's ordeal began when they sought help

for their children's individual issues. Despite initial assessments by two caseworkers concluding that they were competent parents, a smear campaign and a change in caseworkers led to a drastic reversal of the decision. CPS in Mellerud, led by the lawyer Maria, used the original observations but altered the conclusion, resulting in the children being placed in foster care. The original caseworkers were forced to resign, and the children have since been shuffled through nine different foster homes and institutions...with all the separation trauma this entails.

One of the two children, who is on the autism spectrum, has been subjected to a cocktail of psychotropic medications, including dexamphetamine, an SNRI (antidepressant), an antipsychotic drug (Quetiapin), and melatonin. I consulted with Dr. Peter C. Gøtzsche, a global authority on psychiatric drugs and the founder of the Cochrane Institute, who wrote that this combination is "serious malpractice." As someone familiar with the field, I can attest that this treatment is not only harmful but also contrary to therapeutic practices.

During court proceedings, I witnessed Maria employ manipulative tactics, including speaking in a low voice to disadvantage the hearing-impaired parents and questioning my competence and motives. Her behavior was a stark contrast to our previous meeting, where she apologized for the treatment of the parents. I pressed charges against Maria. She claimed to have felt threatened by me on Facebook and in our meeting, without providing evidence. This accusation was used to deny my participation in court proceedings, contravening various laws and UN conventions.

Vidar and Trine were accused of abusing their children. This was investigated by the police, and the charges were dropped. On numerous occasions, they have asked for the case documents. Out of 650 pages, they got 109 - most of them heavily redacted. How can they defend themselves against such accusations when they aren't told the details?

A question that they have asked the CPS repeatedly is, "What do we have to do to get our children back?" The answer has been "You have to admit to your flaws, and accept the interventions we suggest."

They have countered "We won't admit having done something we are innocent of!" followed by "family therapy is not an effective intervention when a child is on the spectrum."

Life with a child with diagnoses is challenging. There were situations that Trine and Vidar found difficult to handle. The oldest child is now in an institution. And the same problems they had, are appearing - multiplied. **This makes me ponder: when the parents had issues, they were insufficient as caretakers. When the institution has the same problems, doesn't that imply that they are the same?**

The situation in Norway is equally dire. To the best of my knowledge, the state has been sentenced 37 times in the European Court of Human Rights (ECHR) because of the CPS.

Research indicates that children in foster care are disproportionately prescribed psychotropic medication, highlighting concerns over assessment and treatment approaches. This aligns with the issues raised in Trine and Vidar's case, only emphasizing the need for a critical examination of systemic bullying in CPS. **When the treatment given is wrong; when children and parents end their lives because of the interventions, it is time to reassess.**

As a social worker, I have seen firsthand the devastating consequences of systemic bullying in CPS. The case of Trine and Vidar serves as a stark reminder of the need for accountability and reform. It is essential to recognize the power dynamics at play and to identify when professionals believe they are flawless.

As Michel Foucault aptly stated, "One should try to locate power at the extreme of its exercise, where it is always less legal in character." We must strive to create a system that prioritizes the well-being and safety of families, rather than perpetuating abuse and bullying.

If you are in such a situation, here are some suggestions.

- Record every meeting. Make notes of every interaction.
- Educate yourself. Read the law carefully.
- Get a lawyer, and make sure you get one who comes with solid recommendations. There are lawyers who are a part of the system. Avoid them like the plague.
- Don't be afraid. Fear is the mindkiller. Practice breathwork to stay calm.
- Bring a banana and a Coke to meetings. It will help keep you calm.
- Listen carefully. Ask open questions. Be curious as to why CPS decided to start a case. If it is

a misunderstanding, questions can help you stop the proceedings.

- If the charges are accurate, ask "How can I fix this?" Play along with the CPS, but don't take everything they say at face value. They are not perfect.
- Don't lose hope. Many have gone before you, many have gotten their children back.

Read the case documents carefully. Especially the arguments for custody takeover. Evaluate them.

Here are a few real-life examples I have seen, and my thoughts:

"Since the parent has been a ward of the state, they are incapable of providing good enough care". If the system is so flawed that children growing up there aren't given a foundation sufficient to become good parents, can this be used as an argument? Is the goal to create multigenerational trauma?

"The child doesn't use a knife and fork, but eats with his hands." In this specific case, the family came from a culture where they use their hands to eat.

"The family is poor, so they can't provide for the child." A custody takeover costs a lot. As does foster care. If the poverty of the family is a problem, why not use some of this money to improve their finances?

"The child has been truant from school." Truancy can have many causes. I have seen that schools rather than dealing with bullying have sent a notice of concern to CPS. Explore the causes!

So - be methodical, and get support. Good luck!

****

Allison, there are many things I would like you to know. But the most important one is:

Love is kryptonite for bullies.

Meet Haakon Ueland

The son of a psychologist and a special education university lecturer, Haakon ending up a therapist was no surprise. He was fed Freud, Jung and Reich along with breakfast. He started reading the bible a year after his father died, when he was four. When he stopped four years of bullying, he was 14. It was his Superman-moment, and the feeling when his fist connected with the jaw of his worst tormentor was priceless. By then, he had read half the local library.

In 2008, he became an ordained minister in the ULC, the same year he got his bachelor's degree in child welfare. In total, he has nine years of higher education after high school. He became a certified Tsa Lung healer in 2012, a celibate monk of his own denomination in 2019 and a licensed holistic healer in 2020 after 25 years of marriage.

He has three children and a dog, creates healing music under his artist name Mancient, and has a solid network.

My dogs have helped me stay sane in an insane world. This is Trollheads Nessi - she is a rescue Malinois with K9-

training on her third - and final - family.

Connect with him on www.linkedin.com/in/mancient and listen to his music on www.mancient.com. Reach out if you need support or a speaker for your event.

TRINE SANDBLOM & VIDAR OVENSTAD... BULLIES TOOK OUR BABIES

Mom
Trine Sandblom

Dad
Vidar Ovenstad

From Trine's perspective:

We lost our children six years ago. And yes... it feels like a slow death. Christmas is just another day. But you know what? We haven't lost hope! Although we have experienced systematic bullying from child protection and from a foster family, who seem to think they own our children, we believe that justice will prevail. Want to hear our story?

One day our two children will read this. If we have died, we want them to know that we never let them beat us.

We never gave in, even under the onslaught of a misunderstood system.

So, this is for you, our beautiful, innocent children. We want to tell you how we've been while you've been away.

We have done everything in our power to make Child Protective Services (CPS) understand that their actions have not only affected you, but us as well, and that is inexcusable and devastating. We were once happy, running around our garden, shouting and playing, but now our home in Mellerud is about to be sold, and we will never go back there.

We apologize for not being more assertive in our demands to bring you back home. We were told that wanting to take you home was irresponsible, that it would hinder your progress and put you at risk. However, this decision was based on flawed evaluations from kindergartens, schools, police and even hate speech from a poisoned Facebook group. Your foster families and half-siblings also subjected you to police questioning on trumped-up charges - an investigation that was concluded and we were cleared of the serious charges.

We should have protected you from this, but we were exposed to bullying from the system and authorities. We know they are trying to turn you against us with lies. They have made fools of us and you by not following your will. We can document that you said you wanted to come home. After a heartbreaking investigation, they should have seen how you really felt about us, but they took you away from our care.

During the investigation, we took a cautious approach, which eventually led to us meeting with hugs and laughter. One of you wanted to stay at Platea and the other wanted to join us back. We respected your wishes.

Two social workers said that the right thing would be for you to come home, when you were ready for the transition. However, the original conclusion of their inquiry was changed by two new CPS chiefs after they claimed the police had uncovered abuse.

You said things about us that weren't true; we think this was the foster home talking, and not you. We didn't even get to celebrate Christmas together that year. But what you told us has remained in our hearts: "When are we going home to Norway, Mother? "Dad, can I get a dog when we come to Norway??" "Mom, Dad, I love you, I want a Hug…"

Although we have had wonderful parties with one of your sisters and nephew since then, *you, our biggest heartbreakers and priceless treasures, are missed.* Christmas is just another day, holidays are hard without you, and your birthdays are days of sadness and remembrance. This is yet another sign of the systemic bullying we have encountered.

We have established that a 1st Secretary from the CPS released the secret stamp pre-investigation information six months before it was closed. One of you told the foster mother that we had not done what you accused us of, but this was ignored. Our ombudsman and assistant, Haakon, a Norwegian colleague in the Swedish child protection service, was lied to in court. This is slander and insult.

He has worked hard to give you the rightful treatment you are entitled to. We suggested that he be an independent consultant and review our case, given his long expertise in the field, and to meet the two of you. This was rejected by the CPS.

We've been told you won't see us or ever come home. We don't think it's true, and the only way we'd believe it is if we heard it from you ourselves.

Your father wants to
tell you this:

My dear children,

You are my two pearls. You may not know me anymore, but I am your father and I have fought for you to maintain your rights.

I'm angry, but I'm not angry at you - I'm angry at the system that hasn't given you the support and follow-up it should.

I see that it is very difficult for both of you to say that you want to meet with me and mom. 'The situation' has made it easier to say no.

When you get older, you will see what really happened. The truth is in your heart, and what you choose to believe is up to you. I don't blame you, nor anyone else in our family, and I know you are not to blame for what happened. I will never hold a grudge against you. I will continue to fight for you as long as I live. I know that when you read this letter, I may no longer be alive, but you will always be in my thoughts.

Please... think twice before asking the system for help. We did, and look where it got us.

You have been bullied just like mom and I have been. This is how I see the system, and that is not okay.

When you were taken from us, I cried. Very loud. I promised you both that I would fight for you as long as I could. And I love you with all my heart and soul, my beautiful children.

We have had our battles and discussions. Life is not always easy. But we have also had many happy and wonderful moments together. I hope that we can meet again one day, but I don't know when that will happen.

I will not use your names in this book because I want to protect you, as there are many dishonest people who may try to take advantage of you if I do.

Love, Dad.

Navigating this journey has been exhausting, and for those who haven't faced such trials, consider yourself lucky to not have to endure one of the most heartbreaking experiences a parent can face. Over the past six years, we have experienced despair, sadness, frustration and anger, but also moments of joy.

****

Sharing what we have learned:

If you find yourself in a similar situation, focus on the rights of your children. Document every call, every visit and request access to the case files. Stand firm in your efforts and look for a lawyer who really advocates for you. Ask other parents for referrals. Remember that it is important to seek help for mental health - we are here for each other. Embrace life, even in the toughest moments.

Please contact us at https://www.linkedin.com/in/trine-lise-sandblom-irdenstam-41b517273/ if we can support you.

Meet Dad

My name is Vidar Ovenstad, and I want to share a story that may be hard to believe. I started using heroin when I was 10, and I've also lived on the streets. I was living a nightmare, but my grandfather helped me with my addiction problem. I spent six months in rehabilitation.

I wanted to help others who had problems in life. A family friend who was a psychologist helped me get into psychology studies.

I met my former partner and had two children with her. She accused me of sexual abuse when my children were young. I was arrested and imprisoned and lost my authorization as a psychologist after 20 years of work.

My former spouse was diagnosed with schizophrenia and put on medication that hurt her. 21 different substances at once.

The abuse charges were dropped and I have good contact with my boys today.

We need to fix the system. It's wrong!

Meet Mom:

As a parent and advocate, I, Trine Sandblom, have fought together with my partner for six of the 17 years we have lived together to protect our two children from CPS, a system that denies us contact and visitation rights. Despite the emotional toll of this battle, which has almost taken our lives, my unwavering commitment to my children never will never end. I haven't given up hope, so I aim to give strength and hope to families navigating similar struggles, and inspire them not to give up in the dark. We can fight the darkness - resilience and compassion can overcome adversity and I encourage you to stand firm against community bullying. My goal is to help others find the strength to persevere, even in the darkest moments, and never abandon their children. By sharing my experiences, I hope to inspire others to hold on to hope and keep fighting for their loved ones. Shared experiences give me hope and comfort!

NANCY O'NEILL...THE UNJUST

Hey Allison, what I really want you to know is that millions are impacted by bullying within their communities, workplaces and all systems that supposedly support children and families in society.

What I want to know is *when does it stop?* The struggle, suffering it hit me so hard during the Covid 19 lockdowns and mandates living and teaching inside the Reservation. I never want to live that again.

Wow, I couldn't even count the times I have been bullied, stood up to bullies and am still fighting against them right now. Holy cow it's like people can't live by the 'Golden Rule,' do unto others as you would have done on to you. What the hell, eh? It's that separation that creates a great divide. It was always there; I just didn't know it.

Can you imagine being almost choked to death over a bottle of booze. Sober as shit myself and being man handled by someone who is 60 pounds heavier and under the influence of alcohol? Or being thrown to the ground and having a large man kick the cabinet in front of your face over and over with a steel toe boot, knowing one blow could destroy my face forever, even kill me? Holy shit having to carry a knife and watch your back from the age of 14, many years later leaving a bat at your door in case my 'CRAZY BITCH' sister-in-law was going to come and try to kick it in. Why? To shut me up. She created a huge lie against my beautiful innocent family. Why have I become a writer today? How else could I share my story?

That's how it goes on the reservation. The life of the Rez, after generations of people living in trauma and being bullied by every supporting institution and silenced at all costs. It's real. I am still inside of it right now. Owed millions by the Federal Gov., institutions and the judiciary are the biggest bullies I have ever met in my life. Working inside Reservation schools and communities will make you tough or break you all together. I had to learn that the hard way.

I was bullied into so many situations; I had to keep fighting from the small town I grew up in Woodstock, NB.

It changed my life forever. I didn't know what bullying even was. It wasn't taught in school and back then you had to suck it up or face the consequences. The bigger girls especially the Indian (First People of Canada), 'FUCK' they were tough. Sometimes they would have a little white bitch in there calling the shots, one who would only see me as competition. And I had two girlfriends who were always getting into shit and girls would want to fight me over their crap. I had developed a reputation for fighting back. Crazy hey, girls and fist fights. I had no choice; they were always bigger and older. I have well over a dozen fights under my belt. If I fought Rez's girls, I was my only backer. Man, they used to seek me out.

There were little groups of them and you were in or out. I fought hard to get in, fight after fight. One time I was on main street and an Indian girl from the Rez just lunged at me and went right for my face. I was like 16 years old. I knew about this girl. She was known to scratch at people's eyes to really hurt them, to win. I ducked my head and just kept swinging until I could tire her, pin her and pull her to the ground. I don't even remember how it ended. But I won, she couldn't knock me off. I would have to keep fighting no matter who it was.

I know nothing ever came easy in my life, especially not coming from money or connection. Everywhere I turned someone was trying to fight me, bully me, steal from me. Wow, that small town mentality. I'll tell you, for me I couldn't live on the wrong side of the Rez. I was drawn there so I chose a life of standing up for others. Becoming a mentor, a mother, an educator. That would mold and shape me, a real eye opener to unseen trauma.

Why the fuck does the world have to be so cruel? All I ever

tried to do was help others and work hard. I got that from my father, a real hard worker. But he always did for others and our family came second. That's wrong, you know. He suffered as a boy. He and his siblings were climbing a farmer's tree and the farmer shot at them. The bullet ricocheted and caught my dad's eye. He was tortured in the hospital, being an Irish immigrant.

Wow the bullying, control and misconceptions within the systems. They have been there forever, hidden. Every system is set up to perpetuate systemic bullying, further supported by the government and its institutions. The innocent are not safe, only those with money and power rest well at night. That's how they keep us under control. The bigger the bully the more rewards they receive in this messed up system.

No wonder bullies exist. Any person who sustained bullying and other abuses is more likely to repeat the behavior. And holy shit when we were growing up if someone called out a fight there was no backing down. I was called out multiple times over the years. Always from the older girls, especially a few Indian (of the First People) holy shit they were always in groups never alone. I had built a reputation, I always fought back. Crazy hey and some girls they just want control and they fight dirty. Those same girls would be bullies their whole life and still are. I haven't lived in that town for 18 years but I will never forget my crazy, wild journey.

One time we were at a party out at someone's cabin during their graduation and a really big chick came at me. It was raining lots that night and we were on the gravel road. She was really hard to fight. She was surrounded by all her buddies. You know the group makes the bully. It's like a gang mentality. We wrestled in the mud, she ripped at my hair and I just kept swinging, hitting her anyway I could. I would pin her and we would be stuck. Twice I was lifted off of her and placed on the roof of a vehicle. She wouldn't stop but, in the end, I won. I was targeted because I could fight and girls loved to challenge me. It was awful when I got home: I combed out lots of hair, was covered in mud and my knees were cut and scratched; bruises would show up for days afterwards.

We were growing up in a time where we really didn't know much about terms like bullying, anxiety, PTSD… shit, I had to go to university to learn some of the unknown. I was already deep into being pushed around and having to fight back. I remember one time one of the biggest ladies on the Rez. She was in court dozens of times for threatening, beating other people. She stayed in our house when we moved to Edmonton. When we got back, she didn't want to leave and had to; she hid the keys on us. So, I went in a window to open the door. Two days later I was in the basement holding my son and the plumbers were there. She came to the top of the stairs and said, 'you're lucky you fucken white bitch,' and turned and walked away. The plumbers spoke up and said that was just like a real 'Jerry Springer' moment. I'm really lucky I was holding my son or I would have had to fight that goliath that day. Come to find out if she got in any more trouble she would go to jail.

She is still a bully and she uses her family and friends on the Rez. Once a bully, always a bully. It's a really hard cycle to break and from what I see it's a perpetuated cycle in communities, work places, schools and households. A lifetime of bullying against my person, I just didn't understand it. Yet it was all around me through my middle school, high school, my first marriage, my job, mentoring and subbing in a local high school working and living in the Reservations.

It molded me into who I am today and pushed me forward in my career. I had to leave that small town and my first reservation. My first husband was very controlling and struggled with addictions. He really had to have his drink and would swear at me and verbally abuse me. He couldn't control it with alcohol, amplified when mixed with drugs. His behaviors toward me came from inside brought out by generations of bullying, being broken in a corrupt system and beaten for not complying.

That is exactly why people do comply, especially being born in the Reservations, where they're 350 years into colonization in that area of Canada. His dad went to Residential school and was beaten for speaking his 'native tongue.' He was of Maliseet descent. They were struck with rulers on the arms, slapped in the head; all common practice. In those schools you had to comply or you were subject to heinous crimes, of abuse, bullying, sexual molestation, starvation and in many cases turned against your own family members. Children just simply disappeared, many never to return.

Bullying as I said is in all systems under government. They thrive off of it in a capitalistic society. If you see a broken person no matter the race, age or religion, somewhere along the line they have experienced bullying leading to multiple abuses, confusion, stress, disorders - all of which gets transferred onto others. We need education, proper support, and removing the sanctions placed on mankind through poorly governed countries on a global scale. I have dealt with insurance companies, lawyers, judges, employers, corrupt principals, reporting agencies, law enforcement, the list is extensive. People need to have fairness and equality in the systems, not what is continuing in our country and others especially over the last four years.

The year before Covid, I was working in my role as Guidance Counsellor and Inclusive Ed. coordinator, with a young officer from the Peace River RCMP (Royal Canadian Mounted Police) stationed on the Rez. Like so many others in my 16 years there, he did a presentation on bullying. It was awesome; focused on students who were in grades 4-6. On every slide there was a question like, Who do you go to if you are bullied, scared, hurt or in need of help? The answer was Nancy (me)! The kids were cheering it out loud. I went to bat so many times for the kids, the community, the elders and at times they had to fight to keep me. It was a revolving door there.

A new Chief and Council could change the whole school and when Kee Tas Kee Now Tribal Council took over the six communities education role under their authority, I was there at the ground breaking ceremony. Their first principal, like several others, was good. Sadly, none of them could stay. There were probably 14 principals over my 16 years. The bullying in the Reserves is rampant. My goodness and what was to come. I wouldn't wish it on my worst enemy. When you stand up for the truth in Reservation their schools, to leadership and try to make positive change, look out. You will have to watch over your shoulder forever. I'm still living it right now and I am off the Rez. for close to two years.

I had to learn the hard way. Four months into the

Covid lockdowns and closures, our children were illegally apprehended on a CLOSED INVESTIGATION # 990227. My goodness the bullying I have sustained over the last four years! I can never forget and won't surrender to their sanctions. Living, teaching and being a mother on the reservation, someone decided they could 'FUCK' with my family and get away with it. Well, they now see things a bit differently. Those privileged animals thinking they are all high and mighty, stepping on the heads of my innocent family and others for money.

My Indian husband says that was the day I saw you break. Neither my husband nor myself had any involvement with Child and Family Services; it is not in my bloodline. For the Indian (Indigenous, First People) it is entirely different: they have been forced *for generations* to give up their children on false pretenses. This continues full force inside of the Reservation and in my findings globally. When your child(ren) are hidden from you, like my 18-month-old who I was still nursing and my three other beautiful children, all five of which I had via C-section, you feel a horrible emptiness in your womb. Until then, I had not been exposed to this type of trauma like billions of people being impacted worldwide with the loss of a child. Eight MILLION children go missing each year. I say that will only increase if we don't wake up and stop what's taking place.

Our family was targeted; Covid lockdowns and mandates made it possible. The grandmother of my step child wanted her grandchildren, especially the one we raised. This young girl is worth lots of money in the system: she is fully diagnosed with multiple brain traumas and silenced in the courts. The grandmother with unseen brain trauma herself, a known prostitute years prior, a Sixty Scoop Survivor with substance abuse, a cousin, aunty and another direct connection to the ladies helped to rip my family apart under KTC Tribal Council. She is a pro in the Child Welfare 'SCAM.'

When someone takes your whole life away, on a lie, holy shit it's the worst crime against a family, the innocent. It was an ILLEGAL APPREHENSION on FALSE ACCUSATION under law enforcement. I felt so confused and scared, we had no one to turn to. Our babies…it was like they were dead. It was the worst feeling in my whole life. We were being treated as criminals and didn't even know what was happening. For five days our children were hidden from us; 12 days, total. Before they were returned to the Reservation, we were made criminals against our own children and false accusers. This is standard practice on the reservations, they implement a No Contact Clause immediately, to break the bonds of the family. You are living in a nightmare you can't escape from.

That first judge was cold and emotionless. He talked down to us when all we wanted was our children and to know where they were. Remember, this was all happening on a closed investigation number # 990227, from six weeks prior. I was in such a whirlwind calling everywhere I could reach. Three days after the illegal apprehension, a young officer of the Peace River RCMP read me the 911 call. It was opened June 6th, 2020, then closed and DEEMED MALICIOUS the next day, June 7th, 2020. There was a plan in motion for one year to get my step child back to her bio mother who lost her three of her children on a Meth Apprehension five months later in Peace River AB. They forced the child from us into real danger. This woman has 30 occurrences with Child and Family Services on and off Reserve since 1998. My sister-in-law and their three children are all with unseen brain trauma, the only one fully diagnosed is my step child and it took five years to get the diagnosis. My sister-in-law is one of the biggest bullies I ever met in my life, and is presently escaping punishment for her crimes right now. The criminals are always rewarded and the innocent are made to suffer.

One of the 2nd worst days of my entire life was when I sat in my vehicle outside the courthouse in High Prairie, AB. I was not allowed in even though I had requested to do so. The only people I knew to be in attendance were the Advocate Lawyer, the Director's Lawyer of KTC CFS and the judge. This one was a female judge and holy shit she is one of the biggest bullies I ever experienced in my life. She and the lawyers laughed and joked as they discussed my children; four months prior she was nice to me. They didn't know the names of my children, when they were apprehended or how long they had been in care. The Advocate said the little guy is getting close to time in care, the judge said to him, "If you want them, you can have them all 'PGO' (Permanent Guardianship Order) that's meant for life." I couldn't believe my ears, all of this happening nine months after they had illegally apprehended our children. This court was a set up. After I did some calling around, I discovered she lied to others in the courthouse and brought more people into their scam. This is common practice and treatment for the people on the Reservations.

Court sitting after sitting, I was made to sit for hours, many times alone, moving our case forward. I had to sit all day and listen to the theater they had to prepare for me. The harder they made me work and the more hours in a court setting, ha, ha - they were training me to see all their flaws, learn their lingo and become a top defense lawyer (unofficially.)

It was so important to remove the lawyers because they would take our money and ignore us. A lawyer of 27 years had to remove a claim he put on me first against my counterclaim Feb. of 2022. I won, so who's telling the truth?

One time, my husband and I were there and the courthouse was full, a sick couple coughing was placed behind us and a young man reeking of booze beside me. The RCMP brought in a convict in shackles and an orange jumpsuit; they had big rifles and handguns. There were like a half a dozen lining the wall right beside us. The judge was calling out 100 names, a trumped-up state of events to intimidate me. I was made the worst criminal on the docket for over 2.4 years and no one would uphold the law.

This system is only met to bully, break and manipulate for dollars. It's their M.O. (Modus Operandi, a term from Latin meaning - way of operating). Let me tell you these systems are all outdated and built on tyranny, compliance and driven by greed and maliciousness.

Oh, and how could I forget the Peace River RCMP Officer who was being promoted to CRP the same time she was helping the Band Delegated KTC Child and Family Services rip our family apart, on a closed investigation # 990227.

I watched our trial judge manipulate every rule book, change verbal statements and use Mini Voir dire's (a small trial before court) to take away defenses before they are recorded in the trial. He refused to speak to me unless I acted as if I were a convicted criminal. They wanted to put me in jail for 6 to 10 years for supposedly uttering threats when I was simply a loud lady who experienced severe trauma from my first mixed marriage. My first husband was verbally abusive. I developed a swearing habit in retaliation for his treatment. He, living a lifetime of Generationally Undiagnosed Unseen Trauma, handsome on the outside and very broken within. This comes with a hundred plus years of bullying, beatings, rapes, murders, institutionalized for being broken at the hands of the system. Wow they were doing that to me, too. It didn't matter if I was born in the Reservations in Canada or a Refugee Camp in Uganda... my God, the imposed implied suffering never ends, it molds and shapes the people into what we see today. No voice, no power, no means for change, kicked around and told by the government we are doing our best. That is simply not the case in my country or yours.

The systems are meant to break the people at all costs. I lived it first-hand. We would hire three lawyers before we would even get to see our children and not before we were first made criminals on false allegations. Can you imagine the suffering in our country and globally? And remember it is all based on greed and complete manipulation into society. Those judges and lawyers, who the *fuck* gave them the right to play 'God' with my family?

It is important for people to know the manipulation within the Reservations has been going on for a hundred-forty years, plus, depending on the First Nation. All of the leaders and or persons on the Reservations come from a bloodline definitely from the sanctions of colonization, a Residential School, and or a Sixty Scoop Survivor and generations of forced implied trauma. The current Chief of Woodland Cree First Nation has been selling his people out for several years. Apparently the money got to him as well. His mother was a Counselor forever a Band Manager and a Residential School Survivor. She complied. I know her story and how she influenced Chiefs and Councils to govern their so-called Nations. Always blinded by the money and separated from the people, sound familiar? It sickens me to know the world has no idea what is taking place right here in Canada and is silenced at all costs.

Child and Family Services, the biggest player in the lives of children on the Reservations, are supposed to uphold the rights of children and the innocent. Let me tell you the largest bullies of our time are the Child and Family Services on all levels and under every title. Child trafficking at its finest and fully supported by government and connected institutions - it's business as usual. They fuel the system, it's a billion-dollar industry, free rape, murder, molestation for greed and absolutely no emotion for the victim the parent, family, uncle, daughter or sister. **People, do you understand what I am telling you?? It is time to wake up to the real tyranny negatively impacting society.**

The Child and Family Services, the beast, the giant is completely safe guarded by the Courts at all levels just like the government, law enforcement, institutions & corporations. The list is extensive and destroys lives for bonus, based on QUOTA and the suffering of others. **I was**

lucky I put my family back together in one year under a Private Guardianship Order, but only because I was born into a "White' Caucasian society. I didn't sustain real trauma until my first marriage and taking up residence on the Woodstock First Nation. As I said, you adapt. Trauma and its effects were not a topic of conversation, however, surviving at all costs was: I have had to flee for my life multiple times. Unseen trauma, a life of broken generations and being bullied around, mixed with substances is like a 'Molotov Cocktail' waiting to explode. It could go off at any moment. My current Cree husband will tell me "You have to live like the people in order to help them."

The systems continue to break the child. For many, it creates a lifetime of trauma, an earlier death, unwarranted suffering, PTSD, Anxiety, higher rates of suicide and a life of confusion. **Millions are impacted by the bullying within their communities, workplaces and all systems that supposedly support children and families in society.**

I encourage you if you have been victimized, keep good notes, learn your case, demand all disclosures immediately, never trust anyone, this is the lives of your children and they are worth millions in the systems and billions worldwide.

What I have learned, and continue to do, is call out the bullies; research; file legal arguments for those trapped within the system for any reason and born of Indian (of the First People in CA) Inuit, Metis, poor, minority.

The Middle and Upper Middle class were targeted just as easily under the lockdowns. For us because we brought our kids back to the reservation and not suspecting what was coming. My goodness what I know will never go untold, the courts are used to uphold every falsehood against humanity.

Our case happened for a reason: for me to bring this message forward and **expose the unjust happening to billions of innocent children and families worldwide.** Even if I wanted to quit, He would not let me. The message is one of new beginnings, of life, hope and freedom and no one will be left behind. Together we shall end the bullying that is happening in my country and yours. It's time to protect children and families together!

****

If there were a next time, well there won't be a next time. I have fought so hard and keep pushing back, no one can go against my words or findings. This case is for everyone: it gives us the tools to move forward and regain our freedom, justice and control in our country and soon to be yours.

> *Injustice anywhere is a threat to justice everywhere.* — Martin Luther King

> *If you want peace, you must work for justice.* — Pope Paul VI

> *There may be times when we are powerless to prevent injustice, but there must never be a time when we fail to protest.* — Elie Wiesel

Nancy O'Neill, AKA 'is this Justice' is a Supporter of Indian (the First People of Canada) & the rights of All

Others! Her goal is to Lead the People by the People, Never Quit & Never Surrender!

With 25 years in Education, 24 years as a mother & living in the Reserves of Northern AB, CA for the last 18, she has had a lifetime of learning experiences that have moved her to stand strong in the face of adversity. She has 10 years hands on experience raising a step child with FASD, ADHD, ODD & Expressive Language Disorder diagnoses, medically verifiable yet unseen in her facial features. She has seen the impacts of unseen TRAUMA stemming from UTERO and Generational Traumas which are simply silenced in society. Over the last 4 years she has completed over a thousand hours of legal research and 100 plus hours within multiple court settings in various areas of law.

Most recently, Nancy is the co-author of two International Best-Selling books, Rattled Awake Volume Eight and "The Liberty Issue" Volume Ten. Currently she is co-author in over 14 additional anthologies featuring over 400 writers. She is on a mission, and will continue to bring awareness, carrying a message of hope, life and freedom!

FAMILY

CAROLYN S. SMITH…MAD DAD

*Hey, Allison, what I really want you to know
is what happened was not your fault.*

My dad was not the kind you see on television, you know like Ward Cleaver or even, I can't even think of another type of dad that was good. Stories like this are supposed to usually end up with a happily ever after. Especially if you have a dad that exudes support, love, empathy, and builds confidence. My story was different. My mind is flooded with all kinds of horrific memories of what happened and all the bad things that I lived through. Growing up I can remember wanting to be Daddy's little girl, instead I was Daddy's little bitch. That's right, I said bitch. I cannot remember a time when he was not a complete bully.

When I was young, I used to ask him if I could go to work with him. He worked in construction and sometimes there were messes that needed to be swept up. He always said 'no.' I never gave up trying; kept asking to go and help him at work and his answer was always the same, "No!" All I was trying to do was get him to notice me and love me. I played sports. I loved volleyball and had a mean serve. Most of the time, the other team couldn't return my serves. I asked him so many times to come and watch me play. He would always say no, that I was competing with my older brother. My whole life was an endless stream of "NO's." When I had out of town volleyball games, I stayed after school because we lived out in the country, and I would not have a way to get back into town for the games. The funny thing is today, I cannot remember how I got home from the games. I don't even want to speculate because, well, I can't remember.

My dad made fun of me all the time, even in front of other people. He would say you are so ugly that he would have to tie a steak around my neck to get the dogs to play with me. Of course, I laughed; inside I was dying. Then he would say, "You are so fat, lard ass, no one will ever want to be with you. You are nothing and will never amount to anything.

When I got my period, he was really pissed. That meant he would have to purchase products for me, an expense that made him angry. To try to stop my period, I would soak in a hot tub of the hottest water I could stand. This would stop my period and then I would tell him he didn't have to worry, my period stopped. This way he would not have to waste money on me. Of course, the next morning, my period would return, and my life did not change. He was a mean, ugly bully. I could never understand what I had done that caused such hatred towards me.

Some of the things he used to have me and my brother do were rub his feet, pick his back and face for pimples, and one horrific thing that, to this day when I think of it, haunts me. He told us his sinus cavities needed to be cleaned out. We didn't know any better; thought it was normal to have us clean his anal canal with Q-Tips. My brother and I had to take turns holding his cheeks open. We would look at each other and make faces because of the obvious smell that comes from that area.

My escape

I had two places: the first was our backyard. We had a large pecan tree with a huge root that came out of the ground. I would go there and lie down with my head on the root. I pretended it was Jesus' knees and legs. He was supporting me through this awful thing I was feeling. Why was I here? Why was I treated like I didn't matter? Why should I stay? I imagined the Lord stroking my long red hair and telling me everything would be okay, and He was with me.

The second place I escaped to was in a different place, as we had moved and now, I had to use my mind to get out of his room. His bedroom faced the West and there was a pasture with greenish and yellow grass. I pretended I was out there walking away from what was happening in that room. I didn't want to think about anything else except getting done and getting out of there. The blessing would come when he would fall asleep as we were working on him. Then we both would sneak out of his room, chore done.

I suppose a certain question that comes to mind is where was mother when this was happening. Well, she was already beaten down by his cruelty and she was not able to stop what was happening. She would leave the house and go into town to go shopping. Mother was a diabetic and very scared of dad. He never let her interfere with what we were doing for him. She knew it was wrong, it's just that he had already beaten her into submission. For her, any type of help she tried to give was met with resistance.

There were other times he would have me come in and wash him while he was in the tub. God, I can't count how many times the soap slipped out of my hands, then I had to go and find it in the water. That sucked!

There came a time when my brother and dad came to blows while my brother was in high school. They were face to face, and my mother had to get between them. My brother would have put up one hell of a fight; however, with my mother in the middle of them, it was stopped.

Shortly after that my brother moved out. The chores did not change: I still had to do what he said, and that still consisted of rubbing his feet, rubbing his back, picking his back and face, and cleaning his anal area. The bathtub washing continued for a long time.

Since this was the way I was raised I thought it was normal even though I never felt inside my soul what I was doing was okay. It always felt "off," like it was wrong, or it should be hidden from prying eyes. Of course, anything that ever happened at home was never discussed with anyone outside of the immediate family.

At the time I didn't know what self esteem was. I only knew I felt alone and depleted and that my life would be very short. I would feel pain, emptiness and confusing thoughts, like how can this be happening? How come there was no one there to help me? There were things I didn't understand; adults were supposed to protect children, right? There was a small part of my brain and a big part of my heart that questioned what was happening. In spite of it all, I still tried to get him to love me, and failed at every turn. Absolutely nothing I ever did made him happy. He was so cruel and yet, as a child, I continually sought his approval.

One time I remember specifically he was sitting on the couch, and I was at the kitchen table eating. He started making fun of the way I was eating. He said I was shoveling food in like stock being fed at a trough. As the years passed things didn't change, he remained committed to being cruel. Me, on the other hand, I kept thinking that each day I woke up would be the day he would turn around and say I love you. That didn't happen, it was the same thing day after day. There were so many things he had done, and was doing, that soon I lost count of what someone would call normal. If there was a normal, I didn't know what that was, at least at the tender age of seventeen.

In January of 1984, I was a senior in high school. I had no idea about what I was going to do when I graduated in May of that year. All I knew was if I graduated, and that was a big "if" because I was in the bottom third of my class of 100 students, I had no plans, no thought of what was going to happen to me. I was completely lost.

Then one day a man from the Federal Bureau of Investigation showed up at my school. Now keep in mind, I was in a small school that was 60 and or 70 miles north of Dallas, Texas.

In 1984, the Republican National Convention was being held in Dallas, so the (FBI) was over-hiring positions. In this case, they happen to need typists. Myself along with another girl from my class went and met with the agent. She took the typing test first while I waited. Of course, the test was timed; no pressure right? She did great. She took the typing test and passed with no problem. Then it was my turn: I was so nervous, and the agent kept saying, *"Relax, take the test and you will be fine."* Well, I took the test seven times and failed, seven times. At the time, the Bureau was not hiring clerks, only typists. However, the agent said he would give me the clerical test, turn in the results and see what happened. He said he couldn't make any promises, only that he would turn in the information, and we would have to wait and see.

When I got home from school that day, there wasn't any good news to share. I had failed the typing test not just once but seven times. So, in essence my dad must have been right about me: I was a failure and would never amount to anything. He had won, at least in my mind that day he had. The agent told me the background check would be started and if there were any questions they would reach out to my family. FBI agents also went door-to-door speaking with my friends from school to see what kind of a person I would be in the event I was hired. When the background check began the Bureau went pretty much from conception to my current age and address. Keep in mind, I was 17 years old.

Dad was pissed because he completed some information that was not correct, and the Bureau had called him saying he needed to correct the information. It was one of the agents from a local field office who called to say he had to resubmit the correct information. I caught hell from him. If it wasn't for me, he would have to do any of this "shit." He cursed more as he was completing the form. Per the information from the package I received from the Bureau, parents needed to be the ones to complete the information. There were times I would hear from some of my friends that an FBI Agent had shown up at their home and asked a whole bunch of questions. "Would Carolyn ever sell secrets to Russia?" they said. "No, she cares about people and would never hurt the USA!" they replied.

Things still went on at home pretty much like I have already described. By this time, I had a job working at an ice cream/hamburger place after school and on the weekends. Dad really liked this because he would have me bring him Chicken Fried Steak sandwich with fries and a chocolate malt. Me, I was so excited, he needed me, he needed me to bring him something. Of course he never paid for any of it. All the food I took home came out of my paycheck. Most of the time I was working just to keep bringing milk, eggs, and whatever else he wanted home.

Finally, the night of my high school graduation, May 27th, 1984, arrived. It was grand, *I did it*, even being at the bottom of the class, I graduated! I still had not heard anything from the FBI, so I just kept plugging away at the ice cream/hamburger job. The day after, at 08:01AM, I received a call from the Dallas FBI Office that my appointment letter had come in from Washington, DC. That was the way the Bureau offered someone a position, via appointment letter. I got the job as a clerk with a beginning salary $11,017! I was finally going to be able to get away from that place. I was only looking forward to what was out there for me. There could be no looking back! On June 4, 1984, my career – my new life – began with the Bureau.

Being selected to work for the FBI allowed me to help others. From Clerk, I made my way up to working the physical side of surveillance for Foreign Counterintelligence Surveillance. We were an elite group of people who had been trained by the CIA and FBI at Quantico, VA. We knew how to handle ourselves in stressful scenarios.

The Bureau saved my life in so many ways. I knew what had happened to me as a child was wrong. However, I could not go back and make any changes to what had already been done.

Ahhh, you see, that was where I changed what the rest of my life would be like. I grew up being bullied by a parent… a parent who took liberties with a child who trusted and loved him unconditionally. I struggled for years believing that I was not good enough for anyone; that I was just trash, just like dad said to me.

I dated off and on, however, I never knew how a woman was supposed to act around a man. The only man was the dad that couldn't stand to be around me. He made my life a living hell. I never felt attractive, wanted, or even desired. After all, who would want me, in a sense, I was used goods. How could you possibly explain what you grew up doing to your dad and then have someone accept you, or more than anything, truly love you?

By that time, I knew my self-esteem was lower than whale poop. I always felt like trash especially when I got around men.

Most of the agents I worked with were men. I felt like they could see right through me and see my shame. There were a few female agents but I had more interaction with the male agents. I felt like I had to be "one of the guys" and forget about being a woman. I learned to curse, act like I knew everything, and had an attitude as if they could learn a few things from *me*. I had to fit in so no one would know that I was scared. I figured if they thought for even one minute that I couldn't carry my own weight, they would make trouble for me, say they "hated" me and wanted a replacement. Growing up with someone who was cruel to you causes all kinds of irrational thoughts.

It was not an easy journey; however, I finally met my "Mom" and "Papa," my grandparents. They were my mother's parents and preferred to be called Papa and Mom. They did not care for dad at all. Mostly because he was cruel to mother, me, brother, and them. He used to wear "wife beater" t-shirts and a pair of sweats. He rarely came into their home. Most of the time when he did go to Dallas, he sat out in the car while mother went in and visited her parents. He was so ugly and said all kinds of mean things that for me meant he wasn't focused on me for once. He focused his anger on them. That meant maybe he would forget about having me do chores for him when we returned home, but that was never the case. He always remembered and made sure I knew what I was to do.

Since I had moved to Dallas and worked for the Bureau, I made it a priority to get to know Papa and Mom. Something in my gut was pushing me into Mom's presence. I believed at the time it was the Lord and even to this day it was the Lord hard at work, caring for me just like He said he was going to all those years ago under the pecan tree.

Mom and I developed a relationship that I had never encountered in my entire life. Mom loved me, she wanted to spend time with me, teach me things, show me what a lady does and how a lady acts. She showed me that you don't have to act like a man to fit in. She taught me who I was and who I was deep down inside, a broken child that still lived so deep within my soul. All the horrific things that had been done to me, well, there was no way I could ever tell Mom. I felt like it would have broken her heart. I loved her too much and there was no way I wanted to ever hurt her. What I did know was that when I had children, I would never put them through what I lived through. I made a conscious decision that when and if I were to marry my values about children would be a top priority. There would be discipline, however not the kind I had come to know. I would love my children, provide for them, and raise them with love, empathy, and kindness.

I finally met my now husband of 31 years in Denver, Colorado. I was living in California and was visiting relatives in Colorado when a mutual friend had introduced me to him. He was like a breath of fresh air. He supported me, loved me, and always placed my needs above his own. I felt comfortable sharing with him my childhood and all the horrific things that happened. He never once looked away or said I was trash. Instead, he reached out and hugged me. I told him about these things on our second date. Sure, we have our ups and downs, however we still love each other very much. He allows me to share my heart and help others, like for instance this chapter.

Bullying is a horrible way to treat someone. No one deserves to be bullied by anyone. That includes parents, friends, business associates, drivers. No one deserves to be treated in such a horrible manner.

I ended up having two daughters; both are beautiful young women who know how much they are loved. They never knew dad. He came to Denver once or twice, but I never left either one of them alone with him. That was really the last time I ever saw him. He told me to get out of his life and never return, that he was through with me, that I was still a waste and should have been gotten rid of a long time ago.

It took me a long time to realize that what happened to me was not my fault. The only thing I did was being born. I did struggle through rough periods of time thinking that I was worthless. Then I realized that what happened to me was not my fault, truly. Dad committed the crimes, and in my heart, they were crimes. I could never imagine asking them to do any of the things that I had to do. They were innocent and had no place to do any of the things I did as I grew up. He was a sick man; not worth letting him take anything else away from me and that included time with my family.

In 2018 dad passed away. I was not there and found out two or three weeks later. I read the obituary and was initially in shock all over again. I thought he could get me in my dreams, you know, hurt me, say that I should have kept my mouth shut. Then I realized it was my inner child still carrying some remnants of fear but that it was truly no longer necessary.

My story didn't turn out like having a Ward Clever walk me down the aisle, but I did end up with a man that I love, who truly loves me and our two beautiful daughters. I was able to get to know my cousins, aunts, and uncles. My life is a true bonus with all the gifts of love I have received from my mother's relatives.

Life is too short to hold onto anger, and I cannot change what happened to me. What I can do is focus on ways to help others who may experience bullying. Bringing light to such an incredible topic means that one day bullying (hopefully) will be outdated. It is okay to reach out to someone you trust and let them know when someone is hurting you. Plus, it is never okay to hurt a child, ever! As adults, we must make sure we stand up for what we know is right. Just because someone has a title does not mean they can bully you. Stand your ground, know that you are never alone.

I had to find a way to finally get the answers about why dad hated me so much. Not knowing was eating at my soul and since dad was deceased, I decided to call mother and ask her for answers. Keep in mind that being near 60 years of age I finally had the inner strength to hear the truth.

I called her a couple of days ago and asked if we could talk about why dad hated me so much. There was a bit of silence and then she said, yes, I can tell you now. She started by saying the day she went into labor the same day as another woman. The other woman had red hair and fair skin. When I was born, I had bright red hair and milky white skin. Just like the other woman who had gone into labor the same day as my mother. She went on to say that from the first moment dad saw me he told her I was not his child. He said the doctors switched babies at birth. She said from that moment on he made it known that I was not his child. Mother said she spent months speaking with her doctor that delivered me, trying to reassure dad that I was his child. He always denied he was my dad. Eventually, this wore mother down and I think a small part of her began to believe what he was saying.

****

I am not sure if this was part of a bigger plan or just surviving to live another day. However, after all this time I can tell you that bullying is never your fault. I was merely the one that was singled out for bullying from a bully that happened to be a parent.

Carolyn S. Smith is the owner of Smith Professional Services. Carolyn established her business in 2009 to help other businesses with extra work projects. In 2023 Carolyn began supporting the Oki Language Project that was founded by Eugene BraveRock in 2020. Carolyn supports the project by donating and seeking corporate sponsorships. Mr. BraveRock' s vision and objective is to connect with Indigenous Elders and save their native languages. Carolyn donates her time and is currently seeking corporate sponsorships. Carolyn's passion for working with Elders allows her to connect with the vision Mr. BraveRock has for the Indigenous Elders. A pilot project is the Elder Greeting Card Project that began in June2024.

Oki Language Project

anoldfordlover@outlook.com

SHARON BIRN…A LOUSE OF A SPOUSE

Allison, I really want you to know that bullying also occurs in families. Spouses, the ones who are supposed to love you unconditionally and support you and all of your dreams, can be the exact opposite, in the form of a bully.

Many people who experience bullying from family members keep it a secret. I know I did so for a variety of reasons. First, my ex-husband was very charismatic, and the image he portrayed outside our home was very different from the one he had behind closed doors. *I felt trapped because his charisma would support people believing him over me.* Additionally, I didn't want the bullying and abuse to get worse once in the privacy of our own home.

My ex-husband was very passive-aggressive. He bullied using emotional manipulation and verbal abuse. The man whose words were supposed to lift me and make me believe I could conquer the world did the polar opposite. He used his words to demean me, destroy my confidence, make me question myself, and intensify my self-doubt. The words rolled off his tongue like a sharp blade carving a Thanksgiving turkey. His words cut through my soul; and made me feel as though I was good for nothing, a useless human being with no benefit to society. He called me stupid, idiot, and retarded. One of his favorite things to say was if I wanted your opinion, I'd give it to you. It made me feel like without him telling me what my opinion should be, I couldn't think of my own opinion, or my opinion wasn't worth any respect.

He would ask me, are you sure you want to wear that? Wear this instead! You may be thinking to yourself, is this bullying? The answer is yes because it happened repeatedly, almost daily. Instead of telling me I looked beautiful, every morning as I was getting ready for work, he would make me question my appearance to the point that I sometimes didn't even want to leave the house.

His bullying also took the form of alienation and isolation. He knew that friends and family were very important to me. He stopped me from accepting invitations to get together, making me come up with excuses why we would not be available. My friends were confused because we used to get together on a very regular basis. They would ask me what had changed, and all I could say was that we were unavailable.

A few years after our beautiful son entered our lives, he began to use him as a pawn in his emotional manipulation. One afternoon, when I told him that I needed someone to talk to and I was going to go to my sister's for a little while, he responded by saying "If you leave and talk to your sister, our son and myself will not be here when you get back, and you will never see him again. Additionally, if anybody questions me about what you have told them, I will make them believe that everything you said is a lie, that I am not the problem, and that you are."

I had to ask him permission for anything I wanted to do, or anywhere I wanted to go. He also bullied me financially; this was one way he felt tremendously powerful over me. Spending money also required me to get his approval. He was classic for screaming at me and saying he had to do everything around here, including paying the bills. I reminded him that before him, I lived independently, was very responsible with money, and paid my bills on time. I went on to inform him that I would be happy to go back to paying the bills, and to do that, he would have to stop hiding the mail and give me the passwords he had changed to our accounts. He made himself the administrator of our shared laptop, which prevented me from changing the passwords myself to access our online banking. He would also check phone records to see who I had been talking to and verbally bully me into telling him what our conversation was about.

He would tell me I was a terrible driver, call me lazy, and accuse me of sitting at home eating bon bons and watching TV while he worked all day. He told me I had an easy life, with the only responsibility being to care for our toddler.

When I returned to work part-time, he would say, "I want your life, you have it so easy. Why don't you go back to work full-time? I'll work part-time and care for our child, which is much easier than working full-time." He threw another jab and said, "Besides, without help, you cannot care for him effectively from your wheelchair." He knew this was NOT true, but he also knew beyond a shadow of a doubt these words he just uttered would be like I had just been sucker punched in my gut.

He isolated me from my family as well. He would make me decline invitations from my parents or tell me to go myself, which he knew that I would not do because I was afraid if I left him alone with my son, he would bully him and or disappear with him for me never to see him again.

He frequently started all "conversations" yelling at me, "I must do everything around here." It's not that I didn't fight back, but it was a losing battle. "You know, I would be happy to make dinner but you relocated the pots, and now I can't reach them in the upper cabinet from my wheelchair." He would yell, "Well, if you knew what you were going to make, I could leave everything down that you need, but it's too complicated for you to figure out what you're going to make for dinner."

The unfortunate part is that I had gone from being someone who was so self-sufficient, independent, and confident, to someone who felt defeated, humiliated, worthless, as if I'd lost all capabilities. The saddest part of it all, though, is that I had been so emotionally beat down and verbally bullied that I believed the negative things that he was saying about me to be true.

One of my primary dreams was always to be a mom. He was very aware that every chance he got, he put me down as a mom and as a parent. He would say things like our toddler is more intelligent than you.

He bullied me and beat me down with his words, what felt like every minute of every day. I had not an ounce of self-worth or dignity left. He bullied me into silence. I didn't think anyone valued me anymore, and I was terrified that nobody would believe me if I ever found the courage to speak up. I knew he meant what he said when he used to tell me he would make sure of that.

I got by hyper-focusing on protecting the one person I cherished beyond words: Infinity, our son. I tolerated and put up with the bullying so that I could stay present in my son's life every day by not doing anything that would upset my ex-husband and make him run off with our son. In some way, I sacrificed myself for the well-being of our son.

Additionally, I was formulating my exit plan. I was putting all of my ducks in a row to make sure that when I finally spoke to someone about my situation, I had the proof they would need to believe what was going on, and I would not have to fear losing my son or never seeing him again.

I told myself that once I knew my son and I were safe,

I would tell my story over and over again to ensure that someday it would be heard—heard not for me but for all the others being bullied who were too frightened, afraid, and intimidated to say something and speak out.

There is hope. I moved forward by paying attention to the red flags and building a business that emphasizes the importance of giving mental health the same priority, attention, and respect as physical health; one where I help my clients rise above their past circumstances to design an abundant life for themselves and their families; one that fills them up by focusing on their abilities, assets talents, and gifts rather than their perceived faults and deficits that bullies made them believe were the truth about themselves.

The family is the base of our society, and the family is where future leaders of the world are cultivated. Strong families equate to a solid and stable society.

****

What I discovered is that bullies keep their power by keeping their victims silent. If you are being bullied, I want to encourage you and inspire you to keep talking and speaking out against the bullying you are experiencing until you find someone who truly listens and will help.

For those of you who might be reading this who are accomplices to the bullying and want to protect yourself from being the bully's next victim, I encourage you and challenge you to take a much more courageous approach. Rather than aligning with the bully, align with the person being bullied. There is strength in numbers. Take the power away from the bully and give it back to everyone else!

Sharon Birn is a transformational life coach, multiple number-one best-selling co-author, and riveting public speaker who helps moms and their children beat burnout, enabling them to thrive. As a single mom to her son and a dog mom to Minnie, Sharon profoundly understands the challenges and joys of family life. Her speaking engagements are highly sought after, leaving participants feeling empowered and capable. Sharon's presentations cover crucial topics that impact today's families. Her work emphasizes giving mental health the same priority, attention, and respect as physical health. She helps her clients rise above their past circumstances to design abundant lives by focusing on their abilities, assets, talents, and gifts rather than the perceived faults and deficits others believe true. In her anthology contribution, Sharon shares her experiences of being bullied in all phases of life and provides readers with strategies on how she got by.

https://www.linkedin.com/in/sharon-birn-9a4a5792/

http://www.possibilitiesrinfinite.com

LONNEE REY... CUPID'S ARROW

Hey Allison, what I really want you to know is bullies are like peach pie, but with daggers inside.

"**D**ad, I need your advice like never before." My father often bragged about his perfect marriage: 24 years and never a fight. That it was his fourth marriage didn't matter to me. He apparently figured out how to pick the right person, and now I needed his help doing the same.

"Tim has been pursuing me for over a year, but I kept my distance – it wasn't romantic for me at all. My visitor visa is about to expire. I have applied for a work visa but will have to leave the country until it is approved, if it ever is. So, he's been my friend, helping me move, deal with my awful boss, and laugh. He's got a great sense of humor, Dad. I am trying to be smart here, you know?" I figured my dad would love that bit most of all.

I was determined to stay the course, leave Australia, and hope to return with a work visa, en route to making it my permanent residence.

Then something weird happened one day while grocery shopping with Tim. It felt like a lightning bolt hit me in the canned food aisle of Kohl's, I swear. He took one look at my face, laughed, and said, "You just fell in love with me, didn't you?"

Well hell's bells, I did. My cheeks burned as if I'd been caught red-handed by Cupid Himself. It was the last thing I wanted to do, be or feel. Our dating led to living together, and now 'hell's bells' were leading to church bells... maybe.

"Dad, there's issues. This would be his third marriage. He says this time is different. But little things blow up into big things that were never a thing to begin with." My voice cracked with emotion. "I don't know if they are wedding jitters or red flags. I've never felt so loved but can't help wondering if this will work out. You told me your secret to a happy marriage was communication, so I'm calling to ask how do you know if you can talk through some of these things, or not? It's been up-and-down, big time. Is chemistry enough to override these hurdles?"

The Great-All-Knowing Dad said, "What's his last name?"

"Cox, why?"

"He doesn't sound Aboriginal. Just marry him."

I valued his insights on what it took to have a happy marriage. Yet, none of my expressed concerns were ever addressed, and so I minimized my misgivings to being "picky" or "uncompromising." What I should have realized is he took the easy way out, choosing 'apathy' over all else.

An on-off relationship, polluted with fears and tears, followed by gifts, apologies, promises to do better, and a love so strong I was willing to give yet another 'hall pass' eventually gave way to 'give it a go.' The timing appeared to be divinely sent. Maybe it was "meant to be" for me to remain in Australia, after all? I personally took-on all our difficulties. I just needed to be more understanding, assuring and cooperative. That's what love does, right?

And so, at age 47, Tim Cox and I married in a little beach wedding on the shores of Hervey Bay, QLD. Rain threatened all day, but the clouds parted at exactly the right time, as if all was right with the world...and this was "meant to be."

"You light up when he walks in the room! I'm so happy to see this working out," said my closest friend, Georgina. Looking back now, I'm pretty sure she was simply relieved the up-and-down affair was out of her hair.

Our budget honeymoon included three nights in the big city. I couldn't wait to hit a real nightclub. For the first time in my life, I had a dance partner and someone to share all of life's moments forever.

Elated but exhausted, I said "I need a disco nap, honey. Please wake me up at 11pm. Clubs don't get going till midnight. I'll be good to git down, just need a small nap, babe, ok?"

It was 1am when I awoke. Oh shit!

"You didn't get up," he said. His ice blue eyes suddenly felt like daggers, not sparkling diamonds. Where did my loving husband go??

"I asked you to wake me up so we could go out," I said.

"You didn't get up. You slept through our first night together as husband and wife. Thanks a lot."

A light sleeper, I knew it wasn't 'on me' – he never tried to wake me up. And there he was, trying to put it on me that we missed the club. The night I dreamed of my whole life escalated into a nightmare. Attempts to console, apologize, and move past it were met with searing words and accusations. I'd done this on purpose, he claimed. Instead of love and laughter, the walls shook with rage.

The following day was not filled with Kodak moments but rather, arguments in public spaces. Our honeymoon went to hell in a handbasket. We drove home in silence.

Daily life became a mix of good days and battle cries. Tim attacked everything about me, right down to the color lipstick I wore. He gas-lit my every move. Making a grocery list was "writing a letter to my boyfriend back in the states." Going out for lunch with 71-year-old Georgina became "trolling the bars for men."

This, from a man whom I loved so much my heart ached

to imagine life without him…and he knew it because I said so, often.

It was baffling. The "king of the castle" came home each night to a dolled-up wife and dinners only a trained chef like me could serve-up. He never had it so good. Maybe that's why he had to kill it? Who knows?

"Communication is key to our long and happy marriage," Dad said. I tried so damn hard to talk through things, but my husband refused, insisting that if I loved him, I should already know what I did wrong. Then, he would gaslight the whole thing, turn it into a whole other issue, and run with it.

What became evident over time was an extraordinary lack of self-esteem, insecurity and intent to harm. "But… but… but I married you. Don't you get it?? I waited my whole life to find you. I love you with all my heart." It didn't matter. In fact, it made things worse.

I won't drag you through the months of verbal abuse and physical fights that included my face hitting the tile floor, getting clobbered by stereo speakers, being taunted and chased around the house until I would break down crying, and multiple arrests – his.

Each time, gifts, apologies, tearful reunions and renewal of our love for one another followed. And behind them, more rounds of artillery fire from the man who once pursued me with all his might. I lost count how many times he laughed while dedicating The Guess Who song, "American Woman" to me. "American woman, Momma set me free," became his anthem. I left him, only to be stalked, scared shitless every time I went out: he'd jumped out from behind bushes more than a few times. "Please don't go! I'm so sorry! No one will ever love you like I do. I will sign the spouse visa so you can stay. I owe you that much. I promise!" He never did.

Crying "a river of tears" mattered not, for they fell on deaf ears. As my therapist pointed out, "You cannot love enough for two people." Lord knows I tried. Apathy is a terrible trait. Nothing can be done to fix it, trust me. Don't be fooled: these people care, they just don't care about *you*.

Thanks to my husband, I was forced to learn the cycle of abuse: tirades followed by gifts, compliments followed by cut-downs, emotional wounds that rivaled bruises and breaks on the deepest levels of a person's soul. Despair, depression and tears snuffed out my bright light. It would take years to recover from the deception and disappointment.

IMHO, "What doesn't kill you makes you stronger" is bullshit. Trauma doesn't make you stronger any more than multiple hatchets into a tree make it stronger. Trauma is traumatizing, period. Seek help.

Years later, during a visit to Australia, I tried one more time to understand WTF that was all about. "Why, Tim?! It made no sense to pursue me, then tear me apart like you hated me. Why?!?"

"Chasing you around the house until you cried made me feel powerful. I don't know what else to say," was all he said.

The man who put stars in my eyes left me with scars for life. Dimming my light was all a game to him.

I can't believe it has taken me this long to characterize Tim as a classic bully. He took advantage of my tentative residency in Australia and played on nerves already frayed by my employer's sketchy behavior. The independence and creativity he fell in love with became reasons to belittle and bully his betrothed.

It wasn't until I dove into bullying, for the purposes of this book, did I come to see him as a bully. Does it matter, 14 years later? I think so. As I write this, my spirit is sad; lips are pursed, trying to fight back the tears and shake the dark mood. I feel stupid for not seeing it sooner. How it took this long to put it all together, I'll never know. Like a person relieved to finally have a name for their medical condition or reason for their emotional triggers, identifying him as a bully is bittersweet.

Knowing what went wrong helps: don't give "hall passes" to jackasses. They don't deserve another shot. Knowing how to identify trouble before it becomes a problem next time is vital.

*Red flags are best seen when you remove
the rose-colored glasses.*

Maybe this 'aha' will help end a decade-long 'dry spell' when it comes to relationships? Maybe now I won't be so afraid to fall in love again? Maybe. It's scary to think a spouse can become your enemy in the blink of an eye. Will it happen again? Will someone else take all the good and turn it into poison? Maybe. I'm fresh out of crystal balls...

What I know right now is revisiting this stuff hurts. It doesn't mean I'm not healed... It means I am human. I want you to hear that, loud and clear, because there are people who will criticize you for shedding a tear over your past. You have already been through hell, so don't let them make you feel bad that you feel what you feel. It doesn't mean you haven't come a long way, already. What do they know?

"It takes what it takes" so do what it takes to untie the knots, even if that looks like a wedding knot.

If you are involved with someone who puts you down, get help getting away. Bullies of all types, covert or obvious, threaten their targets with backlash, verbal abuse, emotional manipulation, threats of retaliation if you leave – these are all signs of someone 'swinging a cat by the tail.' If you see it happening to others, know that it can, and eventually will, happen to you, too.

Bullies are like peach pie...with daggers inside.

Please do not allow their manipulation to become your reason for sticking around for more of the same. Step away. Get out of range. Treat yourself like you would care for a young child who is in harm's way.

Know that you deserve better. If your gut instinct is telling you to be careful, that something is 'off,' no matter what other people tell you, stick by your own side. Clearly, even a trusted family member can mislead your life and not think twice about it.

I have stopped kicking myself for listening to the wrong person because he positioned himself as THE authority about only everything in life. When all was said and done, when I was forced to return to the states, my father never wanted to hear what happened with Tim. He was too busy chastising me for trying to make a life in AUS. By the way, years later I discovered my father's 24-year "perfect marriage" was all a lie.

I reckon he and Tim would've gotten along perfectly, and that ain't no lie.

****

The only way I got by was removing myself from the man swinging a cat by its tail, and getting outside help to both recognize, and heal from, extensive emotional abuse. Moving forward, if there is a next time, I will take my own advice: *when in doubt, wait it out.* If something, or someone, does not feel right, that's enough to go on, *literally...go!* Be wise about the counsel you seek. If there is a next time, I will trust my instinct, not someone else's lame advice that I need to be less picky or more compromising.

Discernment isn't selfish, it is essential.
Please, take that to heart, too. You deserve better. We all do.

Lonnee Rey grew up bullied by narcissistic parents. Bullies have marked the landscape of her life for most of her life, including her husband, friends, clients and collaborative book organizers.

Reinventing herself from the inside-out, she has returned with a lantern, and a laugh, to shine the light on the path for others who want to rewrite their next chapter.

Lonnee has published 10 editions of "Rattled Awake," the international best-selling anthology series dedicated to stories of positive pivots and business growth. She is especially proud to have been editor of the Indie Book of the Year, 2023. Her books, "Life lessons learned from a lousy mother" and "How to Deal with a Dumbass: what to do and say when come your way," along with her 9th podcast, "How to Deal with a Dumbass (a spiritual perspective)," have helped others feel lighter, laugh more and live out loud.

Her transformational writing workshops turn Nervous Nellies into confident writers, speakers and podcast guests. A 15x International Best-selling writer and ghostwriter, Lonnee is always on the lookout for people who want to speak their truth and build their brand.

MENTAL HEALTH
SERVICE PROVIDERS

SARAH E. F. O'BRIEN...HOW I BEAT THE BULLIES

Hey, Allison, what I really want you to know is that systemic bullying exists even in mental healthcare settings.

I t's not a matter of IF you will be mistreated in one of these systems, it's a matter of when. Because the demand, the culture, the lack of respect for mental health professionals, and the power differential between direct providers—the boots on the ground—and management, will always exist in these systems, as it always has.

If you aren't at the top, then things will never be as easy for you, and your voice will not be heard or heeded. I've seen leadership throw direct service providers right under the bus to save their own asses...and to maintain their position in leadership. Turnover at these places is high which means there WILL come a time when your caseload skyrockets as you have to absorb the caseload of whoever quit. Does your supervisor care that you literally don't feel like you have capacity to take on five or 10 more clients at once? Not really...their supervisor has expectations that their team 'produce' a certain number of billable hours. And this structure exists EVERYWHERE, in likely EVERY industry.

Public mental healthcare should not be a high profit business. This is low-cost or free mental healthcare! Yet, profits over people (both the provider people and the client people) always seem to win. Not today! Not anymore! I'm here to tell you the lies they weave about what's available to you for work, employment, positions, and ability to honor and care for yourself well at the same time are just that...lies! To hold you in the one-down position, churning out all the work, but never making the amount of money as the people above you. **Stop believing it.** Read on if you want to learn about another way... another way that actually works for you, the provider, while you continue to be in a profession that helps others.

I've been in the mental health field for over 15 years. I've worked in a variety of settings and with wide variability in risk, from case management to crisis intervention work. I've also been in private practice for eight years. So, my work experience sort of runs the gamut. I've seen a lot of different workplaces. All of them were shitty until I started my private practice. When your employer asks you to do something that feels unethical or unsafe, don't do it anyway, and then complain after the fact. Advocate beforehand. Or just don't do it!

There are so many instances in which I was bullied at work, as a mental health provider, that I don't have the word count for this chapter to list them all! However, I will give you a few to offer tangible examples. And I'm sure many of you will relate.

- Closed door meetings reviewing my notes and what I will say in a meeting of peers and other supervisors
- Tweaks to my verbiage for presenting clinical case studies in meetings (they didn't like how I speak naturally)
- Unrealistic and unreasonable demands, such as high numbers in caseloads, high acuity clients
- Being ignored or singled out or spoken to harshly by supervisors (once I cried in a meeting because the supervisor was so harsh, and it was in front of my entire team)
- Denied appropriate raise for change in job title/ promotion
- Denied equitable compensation for my title compared to others with same title
- Closed door meetings about what I could say and not say to my co-workers at lunch about my dissatisfaction with my job
- Requirements to make visits to active clients who

had been jailed; always required to go on my own, even the first time (little to no support)
•   Expectations that one clinician provide crisis on-call services for an entire county alone overnight, with only one supervisor available by phone (if they answer, often they did not, leaving the clinician alone to navigate serious issues)
•   Inadequate training for providing higher levels of care, i.e. crisis intervention
•   Lack of adequate guidance and support for clinical decision making and agency decision making
•   Being thrown under the bus about a client's complaint about a bill, when the supervisor told me to contact client when it wasn't needed, which generates a bill, which client was responsible to pay…and they also refused to explain it him, and made me do it even though I never dealt with clients' payments ever before
•   Saw upper management throw co-workers under the bus, after supervisors required these clinicians to make certain decisions or take certain actions in the first place
•   Lack of adequate support when I felt unsafe in a client's presence; required major advocating on my part (it was terrifying!)
•   Lack of empathy or consideration from my supervisor when I explained stressors from the job and on-call shifts were negatively impacting my sleep and my health

Is that enough for you? That's not even every instance of bullying I've suffered, and it looks, feels, and is more than enough bad experiences working for other people to kick my ass into gear to find another way. Time to consider my options and start working on my exit strategy.

I wish I would have believed I could have worked two jobs sooner, because that's what I had to do to build my practice, and that felt really overwhelming. I felt as though I wasn't going to have any of my own time and I just didn't want that, and felt like that was unfair. And so many other things in my life had already been unfair (bullying started with emotional abuse in my family system as a child), let alone at shitty workplaces. I already had to work this emotionally taxing 40/hour a week job, and then still another job on top of it to build a practice. However, I wish I would have told myself sooner, that it would be possible to work two jobs (and remarkably still find some space for self-care) for a time. I wish I would've told myself "You're not gonna have to do it forever, and it's gonna be worth it."

If I've said it once, I've said it a million times: social workers are overworked, under-paid, and under-valued. What I haven't really said is that this is actually harming social workers...harming people that happen to be in a profession of social work. Or mental healthcare. Service providers. Helping professionals.

Have you ever felt intimidated by, fearful of, or less than in a workplace setting? Then you, my friend, have been the subject of workplace bullying. What exactly is classified as bullying? Let's get a working definition so we're all on the same page.

Bullying is any unwanted or aggressive behavior from someone who is intentionally trying to upset, harm, or have power over you. Bullying occurs among children, adolescents, and teens, either in person, online, or through social media. Adults can also be bullied, both in social groups and in the workplace. Bullying creates a power imbalance, and it usually occurs repeatedly. (These two factors are what make bullying a traumatic experience for people.)

More specifically, the Workplace Bullying Institute defines workplace bullying as "repeated, health-harming mistreatment by one or more people of an employee by means of verbal abuse, threats, intimidation, humiliation, work interference, sabotage, exploitation of a known vulnerability, or a combination of any or all of these."

Another article cites, "Surveys reveal that as many as 75 percent of workers claim to have been a target of bullying at work or that they've witnessed this behavior firsthand. As a result, the WBI estimates that 79.3 million working Americans have either suffered or witnessed bullying on the clock. After conducting a workplace bullying survey on behalf of the WBI in late January of 2021, Zogby Analytics concluded that the COVID-19 pandemic has only made bullying at work worse."

With bullying in the workplace often being psychological, or nonverbal, rather than involving visible physical acts and harshly spoken words (although this DOES happen too, don't be fooled) it can be hard for people to recognize. Some characteristics of workplace bullying include:
- Verbal abuse
- Intimidation
- Undeserved criticism of a person's work
- Retaliation
- Institutional or systemic bullying
    (THIS! This is mostly what happens

in workplace bullying)

- Cyberbullying

Fun fact folks, (okay not so fun, but enlightening): Bosses and supervisors are responsible for 65 percent of all bullying, co-workers are behind 21 percent of the behavior, and subordinates are responsible for an estimated 14 percent of workplace bullying. And, what's worse, the people who are targeted are often perceived as nice, caring, and cooperative...now isn't that some interesting shit?

Bullying can take a heavy toll on employees' physical and mental health. Employers may notice their bottom line isn't as profitable due to things like increased absenteeism among workers. And in my experience, this is the ONLY time employers, or C-Suite, will get involved to change workplace bullying, aggression, and violence. This reduces employees to nothing more than money-makers for the 'business' and completely leaves out their humanity. These employees making you money, seeing clients to get that 'billable hour' are PEOPLE. Human beings. Who deserve respect, consideration, fair working conditions, equitable compensation as other professions requiring the same education and certification to practice, and adequate support and guidance from leadership.

Did workplace bullying negatively impact my mental and physical health? You bet your bottom dollar, it did! Probably few people know that anxiety (financial, relational, perfectionism) has put so much stress on my mind and body, on and in my nervous system, really throughout my entire physiological system. Some ways it affected me include insomnia and poor-quality sleep; unresolvable chronic pain for 10+ years; weight gain and inability to lose weight with traditional and usually effective means; ruminating thoughts about work performance and following the rules; perseverating thoughts about ever making enough money in this profession; intrusive thoughts about lack of safety at work; low self-esteem and self-worth; several autoimmune diagnoses; dissatisfaction with work and life in general.

What's more? I am a person who was emotionally abused and neglected throughout my childhood. This trauma has lived inside of me, and it has changed the way I approach the world, particularly relationships and interpersonal interactions. These workplace scenarios in which I was bullied only compounded and amplified my trauma responses. In short, it further traumatized me and my system (my nervous system, the system responsible for regulating threats to safety.)

SAMHSA (Substance Abuse and Mental Health Services Administration) defines trauma as "a result of an event, series of events, or set of circumstances that an individual experiences as physically or emotionally harmful or life threatening. These experiences can have lasting adverse effects on a person's mental, physical, social, emotional, or spiritual well being."

From where I stand, I cannot see bullying as anything other than emotional abuse which is TRAUMA. Another insidious piece about bullying: by definition, it's repetitive. Any abuse or manipulation that is repetitive has the potential for extremely damaging, intense, and long-lasting negative effects for people. Any abuse or manipulation that is repetitive is in fact traumatic for the people who experience it, and the repetition is part of what makes it traumatic; it's ongoing, it doesn't end, there's no safety within, and it feels like there's no way out. I don't care who wants to argue this. I don't care which high-level executive wants to challenge me. I will tell you all day how wrong you are, and I have the science to prove it and back it up!

This workplace bullying is systemic, institutional...and has been going on forever, in likely every industry out there. If mental health providers can be the victims of bullying at work, then no workplace is safeguarded against bullying. Institutional bullying may be the hardest to guard against anyway because it's ingrained in an organization's daily operations. In fact, it's often encouraged and accepted by occupants in the C-suite all the way down to front-line employees. Mandatory overtime and publicly singling out employees who underperform and/or those struggling with personal issues are examples of systemic bullying.

That was my experience in public mental health settings, every single one. I worked at three in and around the city in which I live. They have been operating like this since their inception. The people who get promoted into leadership are the 'yes men' who oblige to the workplaces' shitty culture and maligned way of leading others to get the job done. Anyone who is different, who questions current practices, who raises the alarm for safety issues is inevitably bullied...by management. How fucked up is that? You, the employee, is already in the one-down position because you don't hold a position of power or decision-making capability within the organization so you rely on the person who does have power to advocate for you...and they don't. Worse yet! Not only do they not advocate for you (or your compensation, or your safety, or your concerns about agency practices), they actively CAUSE HARM by dismissing your concerns (invalidation), refusing to advocate to even higher management (leaving you stuck in the shitty conditions without options for change), and potentially belittling you for bringing any issues up in the first place, maybe even retaliating against you, or firing you, for making a fuss.

If that happens, it's retaliatory bullying and often is the result of employees claiming they've been the victims of bullying. Because they've bravely reported mistreatment in the workplace to human resources, these victims are sometimes accused of lying or denied advances up the corporate ladder. Sometimes, they wind up being even more ostracized as a result of retaliation leveled by their managers, the very people who were supposed to institute protections to prevent the mistreatment in the first place. And this occurs all the time! People in power are protected, and people without power are sacrificed. It makes me want to rage out!

Where is the safety? Where is the compassion? Where is the respect? Where is the humanity? Poor, unsupportive, misaligned and misguided leadership are the school yard bullies powering over the small and the weak—the employees who are not in leadership positions. The problem is believing this is the only way to work. Believing this is how it is everywhere, so what's the point of finding a new position, or making a fuss about it, it'll just make things worse for me than they already are. The other problem? Believing you are small and weak compared to your supervisor, manager, C-Suite executives, and other leaders. Because in the space where humanity lives—everyone has equal worth and value. Just because they are your supervisor does not make them superior to you in the game of life. Just because they are your manager does not make them more important than you in the game of life. Just because they are in a leadership position at work does not give them power over you, your health, your wellness, your sanity, your life expectancy in the game of life...your life. This is your life! And work is only part of it. So, if you don't feel valued there; if you don't feel accepted there; if you don't feel respected there; if you don't feel supported there; if you don't feel celebrated there...you don't have to stay there. It is NOT your only option to endure centuries of systemic bullshit to collect a paycheck. There is another way.

How did I find another way? I asked myself "What else is available to me? What do I even like about this job, this work? Do I want to do something else so maybe I have a better experience or better salary? But what else would I do? I've spent the last 10 years learning, training and qualifying to do this work. This is service-based, helping others kind of work." Once I determined the part of the work that I truly did enjoy—the time with my clients— I knew the profession was for me, but the environment was not. The time spent one-on-one with clients, guiding them to more effective coping and better mental health, that was the good stuff. The shitty stuff was leadership/management, hierarchy, red tape and lack of transparency, shaming personal attributes and grooming for others, being at the bottom with no voice, no choice, no power, no decision-making or change-making ability. I was done with that! Oh, another little fun fact (again not so fun), my supervisor was my exact same age, with the same years of education, and the same number of years postgraduate experience—yet treated me like I was less than, and as though she could tell me what to do, what to say, because she was my supervisor. This never sat well with me. This was always hard for me. I could not see the difference between us and our skillset, yet I was treated so differently at work than she was.

For a person who has significant developmental trauma and struggles with the responses and reactions of Complex PTSD, these work environments reinforced an age-old message: I am not worthy or deserving of care, consideration, fairness, respect, or kindness. It reinforced other faulty core beliefs such as 'I'm not good enough' (smart enough, nice enough, well-spoken enough, professional enough etc.), 'I'm too much' (too loud, too crass, too raw, too intense, too different from etc.), and 'To get what I need I have to fight like hell.' Basically, these work environments where I was constantly shut down (often just for being myself) both activated the trauma already living inside of me, and pulled me into even more traumatic situations—this is how trauma begets more trauma. And because my self-worth was already low, and my world view and self-view already warped (from early childhood trauma), it took way too long to recognize I was enduring more trauma at work—I thought, like everyone else, this is just the way it is in mental health, this is just the way it is in social work, we know we don't go into it for the money or the great working conditions, we just accept this is it... we will always be overworked, under-paid, under-valued, and actively traumatized, and that's 'just the job. Just the price of being a service professional.'

Pause.

WTF? What in the hell is this kind of mindset? I'll tell you. A defeated one. A traumatized one. A hopeless one. And I know I'm not the only one who ended up here. It's absolutely insane for entire systems to reinforce active trauma conditions for people, yet it happens. And I personally find it even more egregious that these systems would actively traumatize the people who chose to work with the most disenfranchised and marginalized of our communities. It's the job not many want to do, yet the people who choose to do it aren't even respected for doing so. Most folks do not want to be mental health providers, and the ones that choose to be should be supported, lifted up, given resources, as well as safe and equitable work conditions. Mental health providers should be well taken care of, especially by the systems that employ us to provide an incredible amount of care to others. If you don't take care of the medic, who's gonna patch you up? If you don't protect the doc, who's gonna heal the sick? If you don't respect mental health providers, who is gonna be left to patch up and heal the mentally unwell?

Yeah, nobody. Systems still aren't getting that! All of these systems, organizations, companies, agencies think that they can just continue to operate like this, and they will still find providers to fill empty positions due to the constant high turnover. I don't think that's going to be the case, and as the pandemic waned on and then wound down, mental health providers, particularly the well-educated, well-trained therapists, started leaving the field...in droves! Compassion fatigue and burnout are real things. Folks providing sensitive, personal, in-depth treatment to other humans are the vessels for all of their pain, struggle, dysfunction, loneliness, and fear. Plus, we are holders of our own stories, our own experiences, our own pain, struggle, fear. And the pandemic converged the two in a way mental health providers have never experienced—holders of space and pain and fear of others, and experiencing pain and fear ourselves, at the same time, about the same thing, in real time. For years. This was a lot for us. This was hard for us. And yet we were not celebrated as frontline workers during this time. Our role was then, and is now, crucial to the well-being of people, communities, and the world. And we still find ourselves fighting for what we need, what we deserve. I don't know about you, whoever is reading, but I've been doing that my whole life: fighting for what I need and what I deserve. I'm quite tired of fighting. Even more tired of fighting and not getting anywhere, not affecting any change over anything, including my mood, my health and wellness, my life trajectory and satisfaction.

If I was meant to do this work (I think most in my shoes would say it's a calling, an intuition), and I believed I was meant to do this work, I had to find another way. Or I was not going to make it. In career. Or in life. By age 30, I had been through so much shit in my life, starting from birth, right on into that final agency position, that I was exhausted. I was truly tired of feeling like I don't matter, what I do doesn't matter, who I help doesn't matter, how I feel doesn't matter, nothing matters. I'm just tired. Because I was feeling utterly beat and like the life had been sucked out of me (already at 29), I did not think there was a way out. Because the only way out I could see, the only one that made any sense, the only one that would give me what I want and need, was starting my own practice. BUT! To do that, I was going to have to kick it up, expend more energy (energy I didn't feel like I had), work more hours, provide life-saving mental health treatment to more people, to do it more days of the week —and the overwhelm washed over me. How TF was I going to do that? I was barely making it day to day as it was.

It occurred to me that I could go work in someone else's private practice, and that would change many things and give me more control. So, I interviewed at a group practice. They expressed concern about the LLC they found associated with me (I had already done a few things for starting my own practice, but was waffling, it still felt like a lot to do on my own) and I had to explain what that was about. Another whammy of a moment! I do not like explaining myself and my choices to people. Especially people with no stake in *my* game of life. And that solidified the whole damn thing for me! "Sarah, you HAVE to figure out how to do this for yourself. You will never be happy working for someone else, under their thumb, their rules, their expectations for your work; work that is draining, that requires so much of you, that is done in service to the wider public. This is important work. It aligns with your values. You like this work. You just need to do it your way...otherwise you're gonna end up burned out, unable to work in your profession, unable to work outside of your profession because you have no other skills, therefore, unemployed..." There was that financial anxiety creeping in, the one that kept me in these low-paying, high-demand positions because of the "regular paycheck" and "predictable income" (even though the income was shit.) "...being unemployed, not having your own money, not having enough money to take care of yourself (see, no family safety net. One parent dead, the other absent, nowhere to go for financial help, should I ever need it) is like your worst-case scenario. And come hell or high water, YOU WILL NOT END UP THERE. YOU HAVE WORKED TOO HARD, COME TOO FAR, OVERCOME SO MUCH ALREADY TO JUST END UP A PLACE YOU NEVER WANTED, THAT YOU DON'T DESERVE…AND THAT YOU HAVE CONTROL OVER."

Okay, I decided, this is it, decision made. Here we go! How do we go? What do I do? What do I do first? I didn't really have a clue. I had never taken a business class. No one in my family or circle had ever started their own business, let alone a mental health practice. I didn't have the money for a business attorney. Then I was catching up (via social media) with a former classmate from graduate school —who had just started their own practice. Over lunch and a couple of other brief meetings, that person gave me the basics for getting up and running. Mind you, this is another clinician, another Licensed Clinical Social Worker, not a business person or coach. It's not like they had been doing this for years, making a profit, and giving me all of their secrets. They had literally just walked through all the steps in the past few months to start their own practice and just funneled that over to me. I learned about tax ID, NPI, and Medicare identifier numbers. I learned about one EHR (electronic health records) system, one electronic claims submission system, and one agency for malpractice insurance, and went with them, not really looking into any others. I learned how to apply for a business license in my county and how to register my business with the SCC (State Corporation Commission), and that was about it. The rest was up to me, including developing a website, creating profiles for marketing, getting office space, setting up business banking, trying to understand quarterly tax filings, and applying to be on insurance panels. It took about two months to do all the back-end stuff before I could open my doors and accept clients. And even then, I didn't have absolutely everything in place, and still didn't know very much, and had no idea if I would be profitable, I just went for it! And never looked back! And I can help you do the same. I can help you get out. I can help you lay the groundwork for going another way...and be successful.

While the coaching industry explodes, the mental health industry still carries a ridiculous amount of stigma. It's baffling to me because mental health providers, especially licensed ones, have to go through so much just to obtain licensure and be granted permission to independently provide care for folks without supervision. Then we are regulated by a state board, just for the purpose of not harming or damaging the public in the course of service/treatment delivery; and if we do, the public has many options for recourse for a medical provider (yes, mental healthcare providers ARE medical providers.) Also, therapists are required to keep client information completely confidential, unless given explicit permission by the client to disclose PHI (Protected Health Information) to someone, unless it's the therapist consulting with another of the client's medical providers (i.e. psychiatrist, PCP), unless subpoenaed by a judge (yes! It has to be a judge, not a lawyer, and even then, mental health providers have the ability to quash a subpoena if releasing a client's said PHI would be damaging or harmful to the client!), or the client discloses plans and means to harm themselves or someone else. People seeking out mental health therapy are INCREDIBLY

PROTECTED, and have many rights.

People seeking out coaching are not protected at all, and coaches are not required to do any training, any licensing, any certification at all to call themselves a coach and to offer coaching services. Yikes! (And coaching is also a cover for many cults and other things, like sex trafficking, so beware, be aware, do your own vetting of any provider! This is the best advice I can give you.) Many therapists I know, and many others I hear about, are leaving mental healthcare for coaching. I don't think this is the best pivot. Why? It's much harder to start, and then profit from, a coaching business. So, what do I suggest?

Therapists! Listen up! You don't have to leave the mental health field. You don't have to give up mental health practice to find peace, financial stability, and space for yourself and your needs. And you don't need to become a coach to make more money (although therapists would be the BEST coaches because we're already trained in concepts to protect the client.) Licensed mental health clinicians are in a unique position. While we're undervalued, we're supremely needed! There are not enough mental health therapists for the demand, especially post-pandemic. That's why starting your own practice is a ready-made profitable business—pretty much from the get-go. I doubled my salary in my first year. Tripled the last agency job salary by year two. No lie! And this was when I only saw clients in person, at an office, only collecting clients from a 20-square mile radius. It's even more of a ready-made business with the expansion of telehealth, and it will soon be even easier to get clients with the interstate compact underway! It is possible. I did it! No business degree, no business courses, no business coach, no business plan, no business lawyer. Just me (and a little help from a schoolmate.) Eight years in, of course there is no going back to working for someone else, ever, but also, I continue to profit, I make enough to pay myself a regular, predictable salary... without even trying to get clients anymore! I've had waitlists several times and at this point I just can't accept new psychotherapy clients because I'm full!

This can be you. And I can help.

****

I had to find a way to pivot because working in these places, in these conditions, was going to make me die early. Die too soon. Shorten my life. From stress. From overwhelm. From lack of support and validation. From years of poor sleep and unexpected autoimmune diagnoses. From being bullied in yet another situation. From enduring more trauma. Now that I finally realized I have more control over my life by taking back control of the way I work, no more! I will never endure bullying in a workplace ever again. And neither should you.

Sarah O'Brien, Licensed Clinical Social Worker and a business owner of over 8 years, is on a mission to change the workplace landscape for licensed mental health providers. She's been a practicing trauma-informed psychotherapist for over 15 years and recently pivoted her extensive & robust interpersonal, human-centered communication, and trauma-informed decision-making skills into other business to include Coaching & Consulting services, digital products, and content writing. Before starting her practice, she spent 9 years working in public mental health settings, and it was in these workplaces she was bullied, mostly by leadership. She nearly burned out entirely just a few years into the profession. However, she did not come all this way, attend 6 years of higher education, spend over 2 years doing supervised work and thousands on supervision for licensure, study and then pass the licensing exam, just to find a new career path less than 10 years in, before she was even 30! It was time to find better, and leave bitter behind.

www.sarahobrienlcsw.com

https://www.linkedin.com/in/sarahobrienlcsw

References:
https://www.letsroam.com/team-building/resources/workplace-bullying
https://www.medicalnewstoday.com/articles/types-of-bullying#social

https://www.psychologytoday.com/us/basics/bullying

https://www.stopbullying.gov/bullying/bullying-and-

trauma

https://www.verywellhealth.com/bullying-5218622

https://www.verywellfamily.com/bullying-statistics-to-

know-4589438

https://www.verywellfamily.com/facts-about-bullying-

everyone-should-know-460492

https://www.verywellmind.com/what-are-the-different-types-of-bullying-5207717

WORKPLACE

NICOLE ANGAI-GALINDO… THE DAY GOD SAVED ME FROM THE DEVIL

"Hey, Allison, I so regret not knowing at the beginning what I know now, at the end. That as an employee I have rights, that as a human being I am allowed to acknowledge my feelings and speak about them, respectfully."

I hope that you never face a situation like this but if you or someone you know does tell them that they are worthy and standing up and fighting for themselves is the best thing that they will ever do, for their family, for their friends and for employees everywhere.

I'll never forget that moment. The one that snatched my breath away, and NOT in a good way at all. In some ways I did not come to understand that all I had experienced was a form of bullying, thinking instead, ok so I worked in a toxic workplace. That moment really woke me up to the reality that there was such a thing as corporate bullying.

My hand hovered above the dotted line. I knew they were staring intently at me from across the conference room table. I dared not move in my chair. How many times had I sat in this very chair, taking meeting minutes I thought, fleetingly.

"You all have to do as I say, I'm the president of this company so I can do what I want!" He had said it somewhat jokingly, as he breezed by my plexiglass-topped cubicle. It was said loud enough that the eight or so of us left, dispersed among the sixteen cubbies, could hear him very clearly. He was referring to wearing our face masks. We had all returned to work just a few short weeks before, when the CDC said we could return to work since they started getting the wildfire that was COVID under control.

It would be one of many Mr. N statements made over the years that just made me sick to my stomach. "Breathe Nic, in and out, nice and slow." I exhaled my last deep breath as slowly as my pack-a-day smoker's lungs would permit.

During lunch, we all talked about it: "That" comment. That all of us in the office had taken our shot, with the exception of a few, him being one of them, the rest being all managers. That's the way it is when you work for the self-anointed-appointed. They wield their power as if they were God themselves. They look into the holy waters and see only "right" reflected back at them.

My mind strayed again for the second time in the few minutes it took for me to make the decision that I was going to sign that sheet of paper, knowing full well that I was commanding my spirit into the hands of the anti-christ himself. Somehow, during that second trip where my astray mind led me, everything that had transpired over the last four years flashed before my eyes. The actions witnessed only reinforced the treatment I was receiving at this very moment. Why had I not seen this coming?

I'd fucked up and lost my footing to some malicious-minded monster trying to steal private company information. I opened the dreaded, "haha, I'm a virus and about to take you out" email. Sigh…

And that would be my undoing. After working my ass off, starting as a project coordinator with zero experience in the world of vertical transportation, I would end my career right where I'd started, as project coordinator. All my aspirations for that coveted Project Manager title were lost, in a click of my mouse. So much for that talk in the VP's office just a couple of weeks before, where they were working on a promotion package for me. To this day, I still feel it was them, "buying time."

Amazing that I was still a semblance of a person, being present daily to work there, actually. Having observed, quite incredulously, how forty plus employees moved quickly through the revolving door that was the entryway to this company. I remembered asking once, how come all of the positions that are filled here are still on Indeed? The Human Resources manager's reply? Yes indeed, we don't take them down because we are alway hiring. LMFAO, oops sorry, I am writing this in present time and that's just funny to me. Anyway, I heard the defeat in her tone. I truly felt sorry for her. She would end up a friend and ally until the day she walked out, shortly before I did.

So let me get back on track here. Not all the positions were filled after they were vacated, including the woman who did the applications for the county building permits, and the aging PM who typed with one finger but would dictate to me when he had a lengthy email to write. Why would they be filled, when jackass Nic stepped up and kept things moving?

One day, I walked into Mr. N's office and asked him when they were going to hire someone to replace Ms. Permit. His reply? "Why would we do that, you know how to do it now." Really Nic, like what were you expecting from the man whose paper weight cost more than your groceries for a household of three for a week? You know, the man who would later, in many training meetings with you, stuff his fat face with his Tate's chocolate chip cookies and never offer you one?

Hey, deviating here. Have you any idea what role an operations manager plays in a company? I suppose it would depend on the industry. That was not the case in this company. Our OM had one main role: to read every single outgoing email and rip the staff to shreds for misspelling, incorrect punctuation or misaddressing a customer.

"Misaddressing," like the time I called Mrs. Abstract by her first name, Sophie. It was one of those mornings where I was at the PM's desk typing up his dictated email. He'd stepped away to take a call on his work cellphone. His email box was open on the second screen. I glanced over and my name popped out at me. He had been reading this email before he called me over. It read, "Kijon, tell Nicole to show some professionalism, she is not to address our customers by their first name."

Umm..soz, I go back to my cubby next to his and send an email of my own: "Mr. President. I just saw your email to Kijon, Sophie asked me to call her by her first name. Should I have said no?"

That was at the beginning of my employment and I guess it set the tone for the firecracker that I was. Trust me, I'd had dozens of buckets of ice water thrown in my face to keep the fire at bay. Somehow though the embers always caught again.

Like the time they brought in not one but two birthday cakes for the new VPs, or ASS-IS-TANTS. They gathered us all up to sing 'Happy Birthday.' How sweet, especially when the rest of the staff took turns imperceptibly tilting our chin toward the cakes, conveying with our eyes, *they never got any of us a cake.*

Preferential treatment was the M.O. in this place. The

harder you could lay a "smack" on the top ass cheek, the higher and faster you climbed. I'm not much one for puckering, and that face is usually associated with lemonade without enough sugar.

So what is the definition of bullying? To seek to harm or coerce someone (perceived as vulnerable) Oxford Dictionary.

I was certainly being coerced right now, and the one thing they held over my better judgment was my paycheck, which equaled my bills, including my mortgage.

Fuck, Fuck, Fuck what to do? What to do? Do I dare sign here where it states that I willfully opened that misleading email with the intention of causing harm to the organization?

In the end my bills won the battle. I signed, the tears smudging the first initial of my name written in a felt-tipped blue ink pen. It was as if the very existence of my core values were being wiped away. And, in a way, it was. I became a very angry woman. I loathed everything and everyone in that company after that day, save for a few co-workers who had become my pillars of strength.

When the boss said, "I need you to fear me, so I make sure you do the right thing," I did not realize just how far into my brain that fear had reached. It was buried deep within me, habitually crippling my voice, especially then.

Those last couple of months with that company pushed me to grow faster personally and more intentionally than I had in the last four years. I kept going by replaying the worst of the treatment in my mind, eight hours a day, while I ran out the days left in my given notice.

I was about to collapse under the weight of being put on probation for six months, while receiving no holiday pay, including federal holidays (I'm not even sure if this is legal) and, worst of all, not being able to accrue any paid time off.

I'd gone out on short-term disability toward the end of my time there. I'd lost access to my antidepressants and mood stabilizer during COVID and by the time they were again readily available, the medication had run its course through my bloodstream long enough to really impact me negatively.

Upon my return, I sat at this very conference table that I was about to sign my life away on, and was told by the VP and the famed operations manager to never speak about what happened while I was out. They said no one would understand and would only see my bipolarness as a weakness in me. They never let up, not even when you were at your lowest. This was yet another way to beat me down, and instill fear in me.

I looked at them both in turn that day and said, "Anyone who doesn't even want to try to understand is not anyone I want to know."

I still feel that way to this day. Not just about my bipolarness but in life in general.

For the companies out there with bosses and not being led by leaders, people like me will keep coming out of the woodwork. We will keep sharing our stories. We will keep reminding employees that they have rights and should explore them. And, most of all, we will teach them that it's better to sit at God's feet than sit at the side of Satan.

"The one who wields power like a weapon better be prepared to go up against the masses. The world of employees will only take so much, for so long before turning the power of their numbers back on you."

I signed on the dotted line shaken but resolute, not resigned but instead fueled to get out of hell. I started leveraging my connections in real life and online. I asked questions, reread the company's handbook, and researched the labor laws.

In the end, I did not need to do anything with it. I was employed within three weeks within the same industry but this time around, I have everything I need should I ever have to advocate for myself.

When I handed in my resignation to Mr. N, he asked what they could offer me to stay… What was my reply?

Not a damn thing…

They say every story has a moral, so what's the moral of this story my worldwide fellow employees? The majority of people in positions of authority will try to feed you bullshit all day long to keep you from seeking the truth. Sling their own shit right back at them by arming yourself with the knowledge you need regarding your employee rights, and use the law as the ally it is.

US Department of Labor https://www.dol.gov/
National Institute of Worker's Rights https://niwr.org/

Sometimes I wonder how I made it through, how I made it to the end of my stay at the Hotel California that you can never check out of. Well, I kicked the "must have a title" to be considered successful. I defied the unfair rules within my limitations, always toeing the line but knowing that timing was everything. To say what I had to say, not in the throes of my anger but to stop and carefully think about how to shape my words to be most effective.

I also had a very happy home life. It's so important to have that balance. At first, I took the job home with me. That really started to negatively impact my marriage, my family. Once I put them first, it was easy to leave the negativity within the four walls of that place every day.

****

I learned that people in authority may often not start out as bullies but become them because they are afraid of losing their power. Some were raised that way, by bullies themselves. Don't let someone else's fear or poor upbringing become your burden. I know that I got by because while the belief in my core values was tested time and again, I always relied on them. Once I'd armed myself with the knowledge I'd acquired on the law, and started asking questions I found the courage to walk away. I trusted that karma, that bitch, would deal with them in a way that I could never.

Heard the other day that there are just two employees left now. One went to work for the competition as I did.

Nicole Angai-Galindo, aka Nic, is on a mission to show the world that having a mental illness does not determine the level of happiness and success that one can achieve in life.

She is known to many on her social media platform of

choice, LinkedIn, as The Gifted Bipolar Writer. She has co-authored four Best-Selling anthologies, two of which were part of the Rattled Awake series by the renowned Lonnee Rey. At the end of 2023, she published her first anthology, A Note To My Family – I Am Your Legacy which became an International Best Seller. Nic is currently working on her first simultaneous trilogy launch, A LinkedIn Love Affair, which features three individual books, each with 12 inspirational stories.

When the opportunity to share her story in this anthology "Bullied" presented itself, Nic knew no matter how much she had on her plate, she was ready to clear it to share her story about corporate bullying, part of which she experienced because of her bipolar disorder. She is adamant about speaking out about her journey, so that others in these pathetic work environments can learn that there is a way to get out!

https://www.linkedin.com/in/nicthegbw/

SHARON BIRN…VIRTUAL BULLIES ARE A REAL THING

Hey, Allison, I really want you to know that workplace bullying happens virtually everyday.

As you know, bullying is not a topic that people talk about. This remains true when it comes to workplace bullying. It is often very subtle and very passive. In this manner, the bullied are made to look like they are the problem rather than the bullies.

How do I know? From the moment I entered the workforce on my very first job till the time I got terminated and chose to start my own business, I experienced workplace bullying. In my situation, workplace bullying was another name for workplace discrimination. I did speak up when it was happening, but I experienced retribution to the point of being silenced because I could not afford to lose my job and have no income. I am not proud that I could not speak up as loudly as I wanted to bring this injustice to the forefront. I faced a real dilemma: who would support me if I lost my job and had no income?

I endured many closed-door meetings with my supervisor. She called me to these meetings to repeatedly tell me I would look more professional and be taken more seriously if I cut my hair. This, from a woman who had hair down to her ass.

During these meetings, she would also ask me to demonstrate how I would help the students I worked with learn job task skills from my wheelchair. She insisted that I demonstrate how to use a stapler properly.

She asked to see my car to understand how I drove using hand controls that would allow me to get to and from my students' work sites.

When I brought this to those above her attention, I was told I was young and experiencing a personality conflict; that I should use this as a chance to grow professionally and personally.

The bullying continued, and I'm not sure why, but this supervisor eventually got terminated. Don't get excited;

things didn't get better with her successor. It was more of the same. My new supervisor and coworkers would have closed-door meetings that excluded me. In addition, they would frequently stand by the water cooler, whispering well and occasionally looking in my direction. If I approached the meeting, thinking I was supposed to be there, or if I approached the water cooler, they would immediately stop talking.

Another prime example really stands out: I was told we were having a staff day retreat for our team. It was going to be held at my supervisor's inaccessible apartment. I was told that I would have to be carried up the stairs, and when I needed to use the restroom, I would have to leave the door open. They would ask all the gentlemen to leave the apartment to accommodate my wheelchair. When I politely reminded my supervisor that all meetings needed to be held in a wheelchair-accessible location, she informed me that if I did not show up, I would get written up and not be paid for the day. In other words, the meeting was mandatory! When I went to her supervisor, he said he would talk to her, and one of them would get back to me. My supervisor then informed me that I had to come up with a wheelchair-accessible location for the meeting to be held, and that I would not be excused from the meeting. She said that every location I offered was not private enough. She then said, "What about your house?" I informed her I still lived with my parents and would have to get their permission. My parents reluctantly agreed because they didn't want to see me get in trouble. On the day of the meeting, people walked around my home and critiqued what parts were fully accessible and what they expected would be more accessible to my needs. Being young and easily intimidated, I defended the accessibility of my home, saying that my parents designed parts of it to be accessible to my wheelchair where I could do everything independently and left other parts at normal height so they wouldn't have to do everything on their knees, LOL. While the stove top was inaccessible to me, I could use the oven, and our microwave was in one of our lower cabinets, easily within my reach. My parents broke their backs when they wanted to use the microwave, having to bend down and hunch over like an elderly person to use the microwave.

How did I get by? I stayed focused on my abilities to help the students I was there to serve. I told myself this could not go on forever, and I stayed focused on the independence I gained through earning a paycheck regularly for the first time.

I could go on and on about the workplace bullying I endured in every work environment I entered. That would make this a never-ending chapter. I will fast forward to 2012 when I began working at what would be the final agency I would work for. During my interview, I told my potential supervisor that I would need accommodations for my disability. I wanted to know if that was a problem upfront because I would decline the job. She assured me that it would not be a problem and that she was hiring me because I was highly qualified for the job, had a lot of positive energy, and felt I would be a great asset to her team. Things went well for a while, but then the upper management changed, and it was no longer okay for me to swap job responsibilities when I could not get into a client's home because it was not wheelchair accessible. Of course, they could not say they were terminating me for that reason, so instead, they tried to make me so unhappy that I would quit. I started getting written up for my work being late, and one of my supervisors started sending me job openings at other locations with other companies; people started talking behind my back, complaining about me, and saying that I was talking inappropriately to clients. No matter how hard they tried to get me to quit, I informed them that I had never quit anything and would not start now. If you want me gone, you will have to terminate me. A few weeks later, I was supposed to co-facilitate a meeting with my supervisor, one of our most demanding clients, and his family. Five minutes before the meeting, my supervisor informed me she could not attend and I would have to facilitate the meeting myself. I knew right then they were setting me up to fail. The meeting went horribly, and the following day, I got terminated.

How did I get by this time? I didn't remain silent. I sought legal advice and obtained a small settlement with my former employer. Before that, though, how did I get by? I was planning my exit strategy. This strategy was different from the previous exit strategies I had devised. This exit strategy was different because I was creating a business plan and starting to build my own business—a business where I could help others the way I envisioned since I was a little girl. Additionally, I would no longer have to worry about enduring bullying to make a living to support my family.

I became self-employed, building a business that emphasizes the importance of giving mental health the same priority, attention, and respect as physical health, where I help my clients rise above their past circumstances to design an abundant life for themselves and their families that fills them up by focusing on their abilities, assets talents, and gifts rather than their perceived faults and deficits that the bullies made them believe were the truth about themselves.

I assumed workplace bullying could not occur when someone is self-employed. Boy was I wrong!

I have witnessed people being pushed out of projects or cliques because they choose to collaborate with others that the bullies don't agree with for whatever reason. And then there are the people who observe bullying but keep their head down, hoping it won't happen to them and their business. What a selfish way to live, professing collaboration, not competition, and/or complete don't compete, when in truth, they are happy to step on the backs of others at all costs. Hypocrisy is rampant. Sacrificing others for personal gain hardly resembles their preaching.

Growing up, my dad had a saying: don't break up someone else's furniture to make our own look good.

I have been shocked to learn that water cooler culture and workplace bullying occur online just as often, if not more than in person. Virtual work environments are filled with gossips, idea thieves, and business-busting bullies.

There is one last thing that I want you to know or remind you of. One way that bullies keep their power is to keep their victims silent. If you are being bullied, I want to encourage you and inspire you to keep talking and speaking out against the bullying you are experiencing until you find someone who truly listens and will help.

For those of you who might be reading this who are accomplices to the bullying and want to protect yourself from being the bully's next victim, I encourage you and challenge you to take a much more courageous approach. Rather than aligning with the bully, align with the person being bullied. There is strength in numbers.

****

How do I get by? I stay focused on my "why"...why I started my business in the first place. Additionally, I stay focused and put all my energy into my mission and things I am passionate about. I steer clear of drama that transports me back to high school. Life on its own creates drama, and I don't have to help it along. Participating in drama drains your energy, leaving you with nothing to put toward the most important causes. Equally as important for me is my integrity. Being dragged into drama decreases integrity. I focus on the high value I placed on keeping my integrity intact.

The only regret I have is that I did not speak up louder because I allowed my need for a paycheck to override personal boundaries and core values.

Sharon Birn is a transformational life coach, multiple number-one best-selling co-author, and riveting public speaker who helps moms and their children beat burnout, enabling them to thrive. As a single mom to her son and a dog mom to Minnie, Sharon profoundly understands the challenges and joys of family life. Her speaking engagements are highly sought after, leaving participants feeling empowered and capable. Sharon's presentations cover crucial topics that impact today's families. Her work emphasizes giving mental health the same priority, attention, and respect as physical health. She helps her clients rise above their past circumstances to design abundant lives by focusing on their abilities, assets, talents, and gifts rather than the perceived faults and deficits others believe true. In her anthology contribution, Sharon shares her experiences of being bullied in all phases of life and provides readers with strategies on how she got by.

 https://www.linkedin.com/in/sharon-birn-9a4a5792/
http://www.possibilitiesrinfinite.com

SOCIETAL

LONNEE REY...(DON'T) FOLLOW THE LEADER

Hey, Allison, what I really want you to know is bullies and their buddies will stop at nothing to take you down in favor of themselves. Watch what they do to others. Eventually, you will be treated the same way; it is only a matter of time.

I heard many stories about the elusive "kingpin" who was supplying everyone with drugs. I was grateful I didn't have to deal with him directly. Even so, Dave, better known as "Filipino," managed to affect my world.

He would say our "order" was ready, for instance, and the one trusted "runner" in our group would bolt out the door. Filipino's game was to keep the runner sitting at his "spot" for hours, and sometimes days. He knew damn well what he was doing: exercising power and control, intentionally manipulating the many people who were "caught up in the scene." I hate to admit it, but I was one of them. All that waiting around gave the rest of us time to talk. From what I could tell, he was a C.A.: a Charismatic Asshole. Everyone, it seemed, had a love/hate relationship with this elusive lynchpin in the Boulder, CO, area. I couldn't imagine how a woman could be involved with such a jerk.

"There's no way in hell I would ever date that guy," I said.

"Yeah yeah, heard that before but somehow, he always gets the girls. They all start out saying that, but they all end up with him." My boyfriend, Jeff, our group's runner, not only knew the inside scoop on Filipino, he'd also lost a couple girlfriends to the C.A. already.

Through a series of bad choices, I ended-up homeless. "I hear Filipino broke up with Annie. He said he wants to meet you," a fellow partier said. "Be careful," Jeff said, "He's slick. You're going to end up with him just like every other girlfriend I ever introduced him to." NO WAY.

He was funny, intelligent, and full of it: a bonafide spinner of great tales who clearly loved "holding court" over everyone. I was hanging on every word, having the time of my life. Maybe he wasn't so bad after all…

He invited me to stay with him, offering a place to sleep, food, and free drugs. It was a perfect set-up for a homeless addict like me. During the days, and eventually, weeks, we spent together, I fell in love with him.

In the months that passed, I became friends with the 'inner circle" of people Filipino most enjoyed hanging with, or using as a "spot." We were always on the move, and always welcomed wherever we landed next. We were the party.

Over time, though, it became evident he was as obnoxious as he was charismatic. He was unfair, a liar and mean-spirited, crazy like a fox, too. He knew how to keep people coming back for more no matter how much he ripped them off. I spoke up in their defense, which pissed him off. I might be his girlfriend, but this was his business. Who was I to take away his idea of a good time?

At this point, I was truly a "hot mess." Months of stress, little sleep, and even less food left me in shambles. I was an unemployable shell of a person, completely dependent on a monster of a man.

When I showed up at our latest "spot," the host would loudly say, "Why don't you go take a shower?" Everyone else looked the other way, rolled their eyes and moved away from me. This happened repeatedly. Once, after taking a shower, the whole roomful of people did a collective 'pee-eww' and laughed at me. "Go take another shower and use soap this time!" someone said. I could hear them laughing as I stood naked in a stranger's bathroom. I was grateful the shower covered the sounds of me, sobbing. I felt my spirit sinking faster than all those soap bubbles headed for the drain.

I'll never forget a woman lowering her nose to the sofa cushion to 'whiff' it after I got up. "Why don't you go lay down in the other room? Here, let me get you a sheet to lay on so you don't stink up my bed." Once again, peals of laughter filtered under the closed door.

I thought back to a man I once knew who smelled like bad fish. Seriously, this was beyond body odor. He left a lingering stench wherever he went. Did he not notice? Did his wife notice? He fathered two children, soooo…I guess life goes on even if you have B.O. But dang, it was rough. Was this now ME??

I was afraid to be seen anywhere; embarrassed to be alive, frankly. I had so much shame over something ten showers couldn't fix. Once a bright light, I was a diminished soul gasping for air, trying to take up as little space in the world as possible.

Filipino was clearly unhappy with me, but would deny it. There were lots of fights, followed by gifts and 'I love you's.' "Do you want me to leave?" I said. "No, no, just get some rest." While feigning sleep, I overheard him complaining about me. Was he doing that on purpose? I mean, we were in the same hotel room – of course I could hear him. He claimed to love me but the whole group doing pee-eww's whenever I showed-up was tearing me apart. He never stood up for me. The whole thing was terribly confusing. Whenever I asked an "inner circle" if there was something wrong with me s/he would shrug it off. "I don't know what you're talking about."

Not long afterward, we got yet another fight in the car. I jumped out and started walking away, sobbing. He gunned the engine and screamed at me to get back in the car. I ran down an alley with him close behind. The only escape was climbing a high fence. The landing broke my heel, and that landed me in a women's safehouse.

Of course, I was still self-conscious, showering far too often, and always wondering if they were being polite not scrunching their noses. The 'Do I smell?' paranoia led to a tearful phone call home. "Mom, I did some research and think I have a disorder called trimethylaminuria. It's awful, Mom. I knew a guy who had it and it's just awful!!!" She cried with me. What was my life going to become now??

The nice lady I spoke to on a support line offered to send information and an open-door, call me anytime invitation. I was imagining a room full of foul fish odor'd people, like an N.A. meeting no one could stand to attend. Thankfully, that was not suggested.

Piecing life back together wasn't easy, especially feeling like a human version of the Peanuts character, "Pig Pen." I wondered if I would ever have a normal life again, to be honest with you.

After I got an infected tooth fixed, people stopped jumping back away from me. Oh, ok, that made sense. But what about all the other times? I was told trimethylaminuria never goes away. Were people just putting up with me, like the man I once knew?

Back then, no one would tell me a thing. The isolation and ostracizing were damn-near unbearable. Somewhere around a year later, I ran into an inner circle 'friend.' But on that day, with no one around, he admitted it: "Filipino was trying to get rid of you. He said he would cut us off if we didn't go along with it, so we all pretended like you smelled bad – bad fish, to be exact."

My mouth fell open.

"Yeah, it was either do that or get kicked-out of the group. For some of us, as you know, it was how we earned a living. Nobody wanted to be treated like you were, and we couldn't afford to lose work, so we played along."

"Played? Do you have any idea how damaging that was to me? Oh hang on, nevermind – nobody gave a shit about that, only themselves, huh?"

He shrugged. "I guess."

"Some things are obvious, dude. Soo, what are you up to these days?"

He shuffled his feet, looked at the ground, and said, "Filipino kicked me out; said I was stealing from him. I swear I wasn't, but nobody would back me up."

"Uh-huh. Gee, tell me about it."

How can anyone get through this nightmare I went through? Here is what I suggest:

1.   You cannot argue logic with "crazy." Do not try to reason with them. To people like you and me, getting jollies from destroying other people's lives is INSANITY on STEROIDS. It is especially confusing when their charismatic façade includes fake claims such as "all about community" or "heart-centered." Actions speak louder than words.

"All hat, no cattle," as they say in Texas.

2.   Stop kicking yourself. You didn't cause this anymore than you caused good people to do good things. People do

what they do, it is not on you.

3.   Analyzing insanity takes more time than you got, honey. Delete the need to understand, if only so you can sleep better at night. Some things will never make sense.

4.   People who 'swing cats by the tail' are a threat to your mental, emotional, spiritual and physical well-being. Dip the rose-colored glasses down off your nose, look over them, and see things for what they are, not as they profess to be.

5.   It's disappointing AF to find out, and then deal with the collateral damage. Feelings of loss, grief, insecurity, combined with the financial or brand reputation 'hit' hurt like hell. Own it all. You can't let go of what you don't possess. Keeping it real with yourself is the only way to climb out of despair and restore your light.

Betrayal sucks. It can do a real number on your head and your heart. Rumors and group collusion can ruin your business, self-esteem and health...all based on lies and liars who use bullying tactics to make themselves look good. UGH. That's about as ugly as it gets, IMHO.

Over time, I let myself feel the feelings. You have to go through it to get over it...the trick is not getting stuck in it. And sometimes, it comes in waves, even years later. When the collateral damage shows itself again, and it will, feel the feelings. Let it out. It's ok to cry when you fall down; it's equally ok to cry when you get knocked down. It really hurts. Mean people suck and the people who follow them are either weak or "users" willing to sell their soul for a buck. Sorry, not sorry: Ain't nobody got time for that.

Don't just follow the leader. Gossip is cheap. Formulate your own informed opinion. Find out for yourself; pick up the phone. Do some research. Open your mind to new ideas. Ask why before you comply!

When you see something, DO something. Refuse to align with a bully and pretty soon, the cheese stands alone.

****

What I discovered is 75% of a group who witness bullying will join in the bullying - or say nothing. Imagine a world where 75% of people stood up for the fallen, instead. I implore you to be the change. Be a stand-up guy. Be the one who says, "I see what you did. Not cool." Be the one who helps the fallen stand-up again. Support the victim, not the bully, please. **If we did this one small thing, only everything would change.**

Lonnee Rey grew up bullied by narcissistic parents. Bullies have marked the landscape of her life as husband, friends, clients and collaborative book organizers. Reinventing herself from the inside-out, she has returned with a lantern, and a laugh, to shine the light on the path for others who want to rewrite their next chapter.

Lonnee has published 10 editions of "Rattled Awake," the international best-selling anthology series dedicated to stories of positive pivots and business growth. She is especially proud to have been editor of the Indie Book of the Year, 2023. Her books, "Life lessons learned from a lousy mother" and "How to Deal with a Dumbass: what to do and say when come your way," along with her 9th podcast, "How to Deal with a Dumbass (a spiritual perspective)," have helped others feel lighter, laugh more and live out loud.

Her transformational writing workshops turn Nervous Nellies into confident writers, speakers and podcast guests. A 15x International Best-selling writer and ghostwriter, Lonnee is always on the lookout for people who want to speak their truth and build their brand.

LONNEE REY...THIS IS THE FACE OF A BULLY

Hey Allison, what I really want you to know is there are losers posing as leaders who want to stifle your freedom of speech, censor your opinion, and shape your behavior with social credit scoring executed in true bullying fashion.

The man you see pictured here has decided his opinion is worth more than yours. Citing a billion-dollar lawsuit, he has claimed to name you, or anyone on social media, who posts anything in opposition to his opinion about a recent incident. This is retaliatory bullying meant to shut you up because he says so. The fake White House backdrop is meant to intimidate while bolstering his political aspirations.

What right does he have to assert himself this way?Seems more like a bully on a mission to elevate his profile, and profits, in the wake of a crisis. Hmmm. Haven't we seen this before?

We see the same thing happening with multiple degreed bullies asserting their authority over others with fewer letters behind their names. *Kiss my ring, I'm smart.* Oh ok.

Behavioral manipulation
Recently, at a BlackRock/VanGuard meeting, a woman said, in no uncertain terms, they expect employers to act as the engineers of social behavioral change. If they do not, their social credit score will go down. As a result, they will not be able to conduct business-as-usual. In essence, they are being bullied to bully YOU. How long would that last if employees walked out? They are counting on everyone to comply with whatever they tell them to do next.

"Social credit score" is not what they are marketing it to be. Please look beyond the mainstream narrative and see it for what it is: complete control over your every move, giving points for compliance; deleting points, or punishing you, for non-compliance to any thing 'they' say you should be, do, buy, say or think. Think I'm kidding?

In a recent video, a man showed us how his social credit score was too low to purchase toilet paper from a vending machine. No shit.

"Thought police" is bullying disguised as being "for the greater good." The silencing technique is classic bullying methodology. All-too-often, the pot is calling the kettle black. The hypocrisy, combined with 'fanning themselves' as authorities, ought to tip you off pretty quickly.

Censorship is barreling down upon us with lightspeed. It is evident on YouTube, where "fact checkers" decide if you are allowed to express your opinion, utter certain words or, in the case of one physician, share health-related facts. The extreme censoring of Dr. Eric Berg was the focal point of my "Rattled Awake" chapter, "Are you a seeker or a beaker?" That chapter, along with all the others I have written in ten volumes of the series, has been narrated here for easy access to important information: YouTube @RattledAwakeBooks

If we are to stand up to these bullies, we have got to see through the veils of deception. This is societal bullying, period. Social credit scoring is going to be the ultimate in control. Will you go along to get along? What if they told you to put a tampon up your nose? Would you do it? Then, what if they said, "No, now you need TWO or you aren't being a dutiful citizen"? Where have we heard that line before?

Social credit scoring is handing over our power to people whose self-interests do not serve the greater good nearly as much as they want you to believe.

Will you become a minion for the bullies and bullshit they expect you to 'eat' without question? Millions did just that beginning in 2020 with relentless bullying of others to follow narratives created by people who have since retracted their statements, apologized and begged forgiveness for their "oversight" - after amassing enormous profits, of course. If you know, you know.

If we are to heal this planet, we have to begin right now by no longer accepting forcefed narratives and retaliatory bullying techniques. Your local bully, like that man pictured, is a microcosm of bigger-picture problem.

****

The good news is we can flip the script in the blink of an eye simply by deciding to be part of the 75% who say NO, no more. There is strength in numbers. Our collective rising is their biggest nightmare.

Will you take a stand in your own life? It is the best way to begin a movement that quashes these bullies once and *FOR ALL.*

Lonnee Rey grew up bullied by narcissistic parents. Bullies have marked the landscape of her life as husband, friends, clients and collaborative book organizers. Reinventing herself from the inside-out, she has returned with a lantern, and a laugh, to shine the light on the path for others who want to rewrite their next chapter.

Lonnee has published 10 editions of "Rattled Awake,"

the international best-selling anthology series dedicated to stories of positive pivots and business growth. She is especially proud to have been editor of the Indie Book of the Year, 2023. Her books, "Life lessons learned from a lousy mother" and "How to Deal with a Dumbass: what to do and say when come your way," along with her 9th podcast, "How to Deal with a Dumbass (a spiritual perspective)," have helped others feel lighter, laugh more and live out loud.

Her transformational writing workshops turn Nervous Nellies into confident writers, speakers and podcast guests. A 15x International Best-selling writer and ghostwriter, Lonnee is always on the lookout for people who want to speak their truth and build their brand.

Be the change you seek
"Better, not bitter"

Will you please share your story with others?

visit for details:
Workshop @ OfficialRattledAwake.com

COVER ART

Illustrator, Michelle Laaks, did an outstanding job in capturing the bully's impact or intent in a way we can all relate to.

She takes a unique approach, and, like no other, has been able to replicate portraits and the emotions behind the moment that matters the most.

Clients are thrilled with her artistic styling and personalization and custom creations. She is currently working on a third children's book.

As a published author, she knows firsthand how to bring images of life to life.

As the co-author of three international best-selling books, Ms. Laaks has moved audiences and readers with her personal journey that is now fully-expressed as a working artist.

Rattled Awake Volumes 1-10

Access all editions of "Rattled Awake" the International Best-selling anthology series based on one question: "Over the last five years, what significant event happened that made you pivot?"
These are short stories of how people are BETTER, NOT BITTER

Life Lessons Learned From A Lousy Mother

61 pgs. - 25 min short read:
This book is funny, insightful and powerful! The upside of an upside-down upbringing, author Lonnee Rey empowers readers to move past the impact of a 'lousy mom.'

It isn't a 'heavy' book. In fact, it is a quick read that can you make sense of the insanity, finally.

Universal truths and witty one-liners will serve you for the rest of your life, for truly these are life lessons learned from turning lemons into lemonade.

How To Deal With A Dumbass: What To Do And Say When They Come Your Way

Whatever you think this book is about, you're right...sort

of. It's really about protecting your peace. And having more fun in spite of the upside-down clown world on parade.

The people you surround yourself with can either add to your peace, or become cymbal-clanging monkeys, disturbing your peace. The idea is to not have them nearby to begin with of course - that is exactly why this book was written. The author learned "the hard way" about people so you don't have to.